WORK
-FROM-
HOME
HACKS

500+ Easy Ways to Get Organized, Stay Productive, and Maintain a Work-Life Balance
WHILE WORKING FROM HOME!

AJA FROST

Adams Media
New York   London   Toronto   Sydney   New Delhi

Adams Media
An Imprint of Simon & Schuster, Inc.
57 Littlefield Street
Avon, Massachusetts 02322

First Adams Media trade paperback edition December 2020

ADAMS MEDIA and colophon are trademarks of Simon & Schuster.

For information about special discounts for bulk purchases, please contact Simon & Schuster Special Sales at 1-866-506-1949 or business@simonandschuster.com.

The Simon & Schuster Speakers Bureau can bring authors to your live event. For more information or to book an event contact the Simon & Schuster Speakers Bureau at 1-866-248-3049 or visit our website at www.simonspeakers.com.

Interior design by Sylvia McArdle
Interior images © 123RF

Manufactured in the United States of America

1 2020

Library of Congress Cataloging-in-Publication Data has been applied for.

ISBN 978-1-5072-1559-3
ISBN 978-1-5072-1560-9 (ebook)

DEDICATION

To Dad, my first editor, and Sam, my coach.

INTRODUCTION

Feeling stiff and sore from a less-than-optimal workspace? Use a laptop stand or even a few books to raise your laptop to the right position.

Starting remote work for the first time? Give yourself a transition period by working at home half the week and in the office the rest of the week to make sure you have all the gear and tech you need.

Work with people around the nation or even the world? Put your time zone in your profile. This will discourage messages from your coworkers when it's early or late for you.

There's a lot to love about working from home: Your commute is mere seconds long, your "work pants" are pajamas, and your favorite snacks are always at your fingertips. But working from home also has its pitfalls, and that's where *Work-from-Home Hacks* comes in. With more than five hundred tips you can put into action right away, you'll discover how to tackle the most common remote work challenges with ease.

Learn everything you need to know for an optimal remote work situation, including creating a workspace that suits your needs and establishing a productive routine. You'll find new strategies for communicating with your coworkers from a distance, like when to send an email versus an instant message and how to overcome "Zoom fatigue." You'll also learn how to battle a whole new set of distractions. Between household chores, friends and family who don't understand that "work from home" (WFH) doesn't equal "always available," noisy roommates, kids, pets, and more, there's plenty to pull you away from your job if you're not careful.

Of course, your home isn't just for work. Even though your office is now close to (or even part of) your bedroom, it's important to maintain a healthy balance between work and life. The good news is that *Work-from-Home Hacks* has an entire chapter dedicated to helping you find and sustain this balance.

Once you've conquered the challenges of working from home, you can get back to celebrating its advantages (spending all day with your dog, never wrestling with the faulty office printer again)—so let's dive in.

CHAPTER 1

SETTING UP YOUR HOME OFFICE

1

GET YOUR OWN SPACE. If possible, designate one area of your home for working—and only working. In other words, your couch, dining room table, or kitchen counter shouldn't be your office. A desk in your spare bedroom, backyard studio, or basement, on the other hand, is much better. Even a simple work-only setup in your bedroom (if that's all that's available) will get the job done. Connecting a physical space to your work will help you switch from your personal mode to professional and back again. It'll also reduce distractions and improve your ability to focus.

2

FIND A PLACE WITH AS LITTLE FOOT TRAFFIC AS POSSIBLE. The more frequently other members of your household walk by you to get food or drinks, go to another spot in the house, use the bathroom, and so on, the harder it'll be to stay focused. All things being equal, you want an area in the home that other people rarely visit during your work hours. Try working in a space for a few days and seeing how much foot traffic it gets. When looking for the best location to set up your new office, this should be your number one priority.

3

KEEP IT QUIET. Avoid noisy areas if you can. However, noise is easier to control than interruptions from other people, so if the least-traveled spot in your home faces onto a busy street or absorbs all the traffic from the den, don't worry about it: You can always try some noise-control hacks to make it manageable.

4

BRING NATURAL LIGHT INTO YOUR WORKSPACE. Natural light has a ton of benefits. It saves you money, since you don't need to turn on artificial lights; it boosts your mood, energy, and focus; it de-stresses you; it helps you stay in tune with your daily rhythms and body clock; it improves your sleep quality; and more. When picking your workspace, prioritize a spot with north-, east-, and/or west-facing windows. (And then make sure you're actually *getting* that light by raising the blinds, opening the shutters, pulling back the curtains, etc.)

5

FIND AN OUTLET. Ideally, the outlet should be close enough that you can plug in your devices without the charger stretching across the floor. You don't want people walking over a trip line—yourself included! If you only have one nearby outlet, get a power strip (or better yet, a surge protector) so you'll have ample power for all your devices.

7 WAYS TO TURN ANY CORNER OF YOUR HOME INTO AN OFFICE

No office? You're not alone: Many remote workers don't have guest bedrooms or empty rooms for setting up their workspaces. If that's the case for you, try these hacks to create your perfect WFH "office."

6

TRANSFORM A CORNER. That awkward space where you normally shove random bags and shoes—or simply let the dust pile up—can become an office with a little creativity and the right desk. Look for one that'll fit perfectly into the space, whether it's a corner-pointed (read: triangular) wall desk or traditional L-shaped one.

7

CREATE A FLOATING DESK. If you're short on space, a floating desk is a great solution. When you're not working, simply pack away your laptop, roll away your chair, and fold up your desk so it lies flat against the wall. You can make a DIY version with a plank of wood and some brackets. However, don't worry if you're not crafty. There are tons of ready-to-assemble options you can buy.

8

ATTACH FLOATING SHELVES FOR INSTANT STORAGE.
Untraditional desk options, like the floating desk or folding
table, help you maximize your space—but leave nowhere to
put your papers, desk accessories, or anything else you like
to keep close at hand. Floating shelves might be the answer.
Install two to six around your workspace (making sure they're
wide enough to support what you'll be putting on them) and
get some decorative boxes to house your supplies.

9

CONVERT A BOOKSHELF INTO A FOLDOUT DESK. This
hack is basically the Murphy bed of desks. All you need is a
bookshelf, hinges, brackets, a stable plank of wood that's big
enough for your daily work supplies, and, most importantly, some elbow grease. First, make sure your bookshelf can
accommodate your desk when it's folded flat (you might need
to consider removing or adjusting a few shelves). Next, make
sure the bookshelf is firmly secured to the wall. If it's not, the
weight of the desk will pull the bookshelf forward...and that's
exactly as dangerous as it sounds. Finally, install the plank
desk using hinges and brackets so it can swing out and back in
again. Voilà, you've got a desk that can appear and disappear
like magic.

10

INSTALL A STORAGE UNIT WITH A FOLDING TABLE. To get the benefits of a DIY bookshelf/desk without actually *doing it yourself*, buy a preconfigured option. IKEA's IVAR model is less than $150 and offers several shelves, hooks, and space for two or three people to sit comfortably when the table-desk is extended. When you're not working, simply flip the table back into place. Everything you're storing will be cleverly tucked out of sight. Better yet, you'll free up all the space the desk was occupying.

11

PUT YOUR DESK UNDER A STAIRCASE. That nook under the stairs can make a perfect quasi-office. Unless you've got a ton of construction experience under your belt, it's a good idea to hire a professional. They can clear out the necessary space (which may require taking it down to the studs) and re-cover it. Add wallpaper or paint to make this space look nice and differentiate it from the rest of the room. After that, you'll want to add a desk and chair. There may even be room for some storage.

12

CONSIDER THE "OFFICE SHED." Remote workers with a backyard might want to take this route: You'll get your own space to work with zero distractions and even a quick commute that'll help you maintain work-life balance. If you're willing to roll up your sleeves, you can build an office shed yourself. Alternatively, preconfigured sheds are available online. Want a custom design without any DIY? For a price, you can work with a vendor to design your dream office studio.

. . .

13

MAKE THE TRANSITION SLOWLY TO MAKE SURE YOU ACTUALLY HAVE EVERYTHING YOU NEED. New to remote work? The transition from in-person working to remote can be jarring, and it'll be tougher if your company office has lots of supplies and software that your new one does not. To get a full list of what you'll need to successfully work from home, go to the in-person office for a day or two and catalog all the equipment you use—from your chair and printer to data analysis software and note-taking app. If this isn't an option, ask a coworker and/or your boss if they have any suggestions for what you'll need.

14

TIDY UP YOUR WORKSPACE BEFORE YOU CALL IT A DAY. When you go to an office, you can leave your messy home, well, at home. Not so for remote workers. And this is a problem, because working in a messy space zaps your concentration. Research shows clutter can trigger the release of cortisol (the stress hormone). Messy homes are also linked to increased procrastination. Before you clock out each night, spend five minutes putting things away, organizing your papers, and removing dirty glasses. You'll appreciate your efforts when you sit down to your desk the next morning.

15

DESIGNATE A "JUNK DRAWER" SO YOU CAN IMMEDIATELY SWEEP MISCELLANEOUS STUFF OUT OF VIEW. Not ready to do a full desk cleanup every day? This hack is for you. If you have a desk, use one of the top drawers—that way, you can literally sweep detritus off your desk. If you're working at a drawer-less desk or table, buy a tray, bowl, or box. You might be thinking, *Doesn't this hack just move the mess?* Yep! And that's a good thing because it'll trick your mind into thinking your space is clean. As a result, you'll feel calmer and more focused. Here's the key: Every few days (depending on how quickly your junk drawer fills up), you need to schedule some time to completely empty it out. Toss what you don't need, store items you'll need later, and put random papers and notes into the appropriate file.

16

PUT ALL OF YOUR PAPERS INTO A FILING CABINET. If your job requires a lot of paperwork, a filing cabinet is a critical element of the work-from-home office. It helps you keep track of your papers, letters, and more—basically forcing you to get organized. Rather than hunting through stacks of loose papers for the one you need, simply open your file cabinet, find the appropriate file, and pull out the document. And if you care about aesthetics, good news: Filing cabinet design has come a long way since the boring boxes of yore. Look for a filing cabinet in a cheerful color like yellow or blue, or find one in a material that matches your décor, like wood or even cloth.

17

CREATE A PERSONALIZED FILING SYSTEM SO YOU CAN EASILY FIND WHAT YOU NEED, WHEN YOU NEED IT. The best way to file your papers is the way that works for you. Many people organize files alphabetically or by date. However, you can also try filing by document type (personal, professional, etc.), person (you, your partner, your kids, your parents, etc.), importance (high-priority files at the front, followed by medium- and then low-priority ones), action (files you need to do something with, like bills or unfinished paperwork versus historical records), or some combination thereof.

18

TAKE YOUR SYSTEM TO THE NEXT LEVEL WITH HANGING FILES, COLOR CODES, TABS, AND MORE. Purchasing a few additional supplies will make your organizational system even easier to maintain and navigate. Divide file sections with hanging files, which stretch across your file cabinet so they don't slip and slide around. Give each file category a color so that you can easily see which files belong to which section at a glance. (This will also make your filing system easier on the eyes.) Label each file to make organizing them and tracking down the right one quicker. Most files come with precut paper tabs, but you can also use a label maker or stickers, or get creative with some pens, paper, and scissors to create your own system.

19

USE AN INEXPENSIVE PAPER SCREEN TO CORDON OFF YOUR WORKING AREA. Once you're clocking out for the day, fold up the screen. Visually changing your workspace, even if it's subtle, helps your mind distinguish between the two parts of your day. A screen helps you create a divide between your workspace and the rest of your home—not to mention, it filters out distracting sounds like your partner watching TV, your kids playing hide-and-seek, your roommates cooking a five-course meal...you get the picture.

20

MAKE SURE YOUR DESK IS THE RIGHT SIZE. Believe it or not, all desks aren't created equal. You should be able to sit up straight, with your eyes ahead (not down) and your feet firmly planted on the floor. If you already have a desk, and it's not the perfect size, adjust your chair, laptop height, and/or feet's distance from the floor. Fitting your setup to your height will help you avoid aches and pains and improve your concentration.

21

BUY A STANDING DESK. If you're in the market for a new desk, an adjustable or standing model is well worth the investment. (Most fall into the $400–$1,200 range.) Not only can you shift from sitting to standing and back again depending on your energy levels, how your body feels, and what you're working on, but you can also customize the height perfectly to your own. If you're feeling fancy, get a desk with customizable height presets. That way, you don't have to find the right level every time. And no matter what, make sure that the desk you choose can accommodate everything you currently keep (or want to keep) on your desk: keyboard, mouse, jar of pens and pencils, beverages, and so on.

22

GET THE FLEXIBILITY OF A STANDING DESK (WITHOUT THE PRICE TAG!) WITH A STANDING DESK CONVERTER. These units are usually around $150–$500. They go on top of your existing desk and support your computer, mouse, keyboard, and sometimes even your second monitor. You can adjust the height of the workstation up and down, making it easy to sit or stand. Converters are typically much less expensive than true standing desks; plus, they take up less space. And if you want to take your work on the road, a lightweight standing desk converter is usually portable.

23

"ERGONOMIZE" YOUR SETUP TO BOOST YOUR COMFORT LEVELS AND PHYSICAL HEALTH. Lower back pain. Neck stiffness. Sore muscles. Sound familiar? Your desk setup might be to blame. To make working as minimally taxing on your body as possible, follow these guidelines: When looking straight ahead, your eyes should fall on the top of your laptop screen. When your eyes are cast slightly down, they should hit the middle of the screen. Position your screen around twenty inches (a little more than a foot and a half) from your face.

24

GET A STANDING DESK MAT. Don't forget your feet! You may have seen or used a standing desk or "anti-fatigue" mat at the kitchen sink, in a workspace, or anywhere that calls for long periods of standing. A standing desk mat will put a few layers of support between you and the floor, making it much more comfortable to stand for thirty-plus minutes. Some mats even offer "topographical" textures so you can give yourself a mini foot massage while you work.

25

IMPROVE YOUR PRODUCTIVITY AND OVERALL STAMINA WITH A WELL-DESIGNED OFFICE CHAIR. Look for one that's billed as "ergonomic," which typically means you can adjust the seat's height, depth, and armrests. Proper back support is also crucial so you can sit comfortably for hours at a time. Some chairs will even let you adjust the lumbar support so it's perfectly positioned on your lower back. A good ergonomic chair will run you between $400 and $2,000.

26

KEEP ON ROLLING WITH A PLASTIC CHAIR MAT. So you've got yourself a brand-new office chair...only to find that the wheels won't roll properly on your carpeted floors. The solution is easy: Get a plastic chair mat. Place the mat at your desk, and you'll be able to roll around easily within its area. This is also a great hack for keeping the carpet clean around your desk—it's much easier to wipe up a spill from plastic than carpet when you accidentally knock your coffee mug off the desk. Depending on the size you want, you can get a plastic chair mat for as little as $25.

27

UPGRADE YOUR KEYBOARD. Type a lot? Using your laptop's built-in keyboard can take a toll on your wrists, back, and neck, since it forces your hands into an unnatural position. To avoid aches and potential injuries, consider investing in a separate keyboard—preferably an ergonomic one. Typically, ergonomic keyboards are split into two sections and their keys are rotated around 75 degrees. That means that unlike regular keyboards, the keys actually tilt *away* from you, instead of facing you straight on. Ergonomic keyboards might look weird (and take a few weeks to get used to), but they'll allow your hands and forearms to rest naturally. Your body will thank you.

28

DIY YOUR OWN "ERGONOMIC CHAIR" WITH A FOOT-REST AND A LUMBAR PILLOW. If you're just starting to work from home, an ergonomic chair might not be in the budget. But for less than $200, you can replicate the most important functions of an ergonomic chair: leg and back support. Get a footrest that lets you plant your feet with a 90-degree angle at the knee. It should be firm enough to hold its shape—if it's too soft, your feet will feel as if they're constantly sinking. Some footrests are even rockable—perfect if you're a fidgety sitter or like to burn off energy while you think. The lumbar pillow, meanwhile, should slip over your chair so it rests at your lower back. In addition to cradling your back so you can sit in comfort the whole workday, it will also improve your posture. Get a pillow in a breathable fabric so it doesn't heat up too much.

29

ELEVATE YOUR LAPTOP TO IMPROVE YOUR POSTURE. Positioning your laptop a few inches from the table will help you sit up straight and avoid painful hunching in your shoulders and back. A good laptop stand will let you adjust its height and angle to your preference and look stylish to boot. Look for a stand you can easily carry around—bonus points if its height is adjustable. For a low-budget alternative, stack a few books or repurpose a cardboard box.

30

COPY PRO GAMERS. At least for your computer mouse. Elite video game players invest in high-quality desktop mice, and you should too. An ergonomic, well-designed mouse will help you avoid carpal tunnel *and* boost your productivity. It's especially important if you're a designer, architect, or other type of creative who's frequently clicking around in programs like Photoshop. Skip the wireless mouse; it looks cool, but it won't be as fast or accurate as a wired one. And unless you want a special pad, choose an optical mouse over a laser mouse—it's more reliable.

31

KEEP YOUR WRISTS HAPPY WITH A WRIST PAD. A wrist pad or rest sits underneath your wrists while you type or use a mouse. It reduces the amount of pressure on your hands, which makes you more comfortable day to day and reduces the long-term risk of carpal tunnel and tenosynovitis. Get a durable one that won't deflate—memory foam or a foam/gel combination are both reliable materials—and will let your hands float freely above your wrists when you work. If you tend to eat or drink at your desk, consider looking for a water-proof wrist pad to protect against spills.

32

TIME YOUR LIGHTING TO YOUR SCHEDULE WITH SMART LIGHTS. Thanks to smart bulbs, switches, wall panels, and light strips, you can design a lighting setup that's perfect for your work-from-home needs. This is especially helpful if you find yourself forgetting to turn off the lights at the end of the workday or if getting up to turn the light on in the evening breaks your flow of concentration. The most basic option is a smart light bulb, which is available for as little as $10. Install one in your office or workspace, then set it to go on when your workday typically begins and off when it typically ends. On the pricier end, you'll find light bulbs that change colors; respond to voice commands via Alexa, Siri, Google, Nest, and more; and even turn on and off using automated workflows. Start with one or two bulbs and build out your setup from there.

33

TURN OFF YOUR OVERHEAD LIGHT. To save energy and create an optimal working environment, use a combination of natural light and lamps. These light sources are diffused, meaning they're less harsh than ceiling lights. Natural lights and lamps not bright enough on their own? Invest in an incandescent or halogen light and dimmer switch so you can put your ceiling light on low—which will give the room a soft glow without straining your eyes.

34

LIGHT UP YOUR SPACE WITH LAMPS. When your parents told you to turn a light on so you didn't ruin your eyes...they were actually onto something. A lamp will prevent eye fatigue and make it easier to focus on your screen when it's dark. When you're lamp shopping, prioritize flexibility (meaning you can adjust the lamp's direction and height). If you're watching your spending, a desk lamp will give you more bang for your buck. However, if you can swing it, buy both a desk and a floor lamp. The more light sources you have, the easier it'll be to create the perfect lighting environment for any task or time of day.

35

GET RID OF GLARE BY PAINTING YOUR OFFICE. Unsurprisingly, it's hard to work when you can barely see what you're working on. If you've tried all the obvious solutions for reducing distracting glare (like readjusting your lighting situation), it's time to take a look at your walls. You'll want to avoid shiny walls, which may reflect light *too* well. Instead, paint your walls in soft, matte hues. As a side benefit, any color in this category will also help you stay calm.

36

SUPERCHARGE YOUR PRODUCTIVITY WITH A SECOND MONITOR. You'll have twice as much screen real estate to consult documents and spreadsheets, stay on top of incoming emails and chat messages, look at multiple website pages at once, and more. If you frequently find yourself tabbing between different windows or bringing data from one source into another, a second monitor will be a game changer. Don't be scared off by how technical it sounds: Getting up and running with a dual monitor takes less than five minutes. Once you've set it up, you can simply drag and drop windows from your main screen onto the second one using your mouse.

37

RAISE YOUR MONITOR INTO THE PERFECT SPOT WITH A MONITOR ARM. Quick test: Is your screen at roughly arm's length from you—and you don't need to crane your neck or hunch your back to see it? If you don't pass the test, a monitor arm will help. Once you've mounted it to your screen, you can adjust its height, position, and tilt to the optimal spot. Adjust it every time you change your desk's height (like when you go from standing to sitting). Your neck, back, and eyes will feel as fresh at the end of the day as they do at the start. On top of that, elevating your screen will help you save valuable desk real estate.

38

DIY A SECOND SCREEN USING YOUR TV. Only need to use a second screen once in a blue moon? Your TV will work. It's easiest if you have a streaming device, like Chromecast or Roku: Just set yourself up in front of your TV, cast your screen, and go. Alternatively, connect your computer to your TV using an HDMI or DP cable.

39

GET A LAPTOP WITH A GOOD BUILT-IN CAMERA. There's no doubt about it. If you're planning to work from home, you'll need a webcam for video calls. While most computers sold these days come with webcams, quality varies. The standard webcam resolution is 720p; if you want a sharper, clearer image, look for a computer with 1080p. Some webcams go up to 4K, for a hefty price—but fortunately for your wallet, this quality isn't necessary unless you're streaming video professionally.

40

KEEP CORDS ORGANIZED WITH CABLE TIES. With all this equipment, you're going to have a lot of cords. Prevent them from getting tangled together, keep track of which cord leads to what, make sure no one trips, and make your space look cleaner with cable ties. These are typically sold in packs, so you can get enough for your entire home. They allow you to quickly loop several cords together for instant organization.

41

CONSIDER INVESTING IN A SEPARATE WEBCAM. If you're frequently on video calls, you can buy a top-notch webcam that'll attach to your laptop. A good webcam offers much higher-quality video than the default one on your laptop, thanks to high definition, white balance, autofocus, and more. TL;DR: You'll look great on camera. Look for a webcam with a 30–60 frames per second rate, which will keep your video stable. Some webcams even offer light rings, options to add filters and blur your background, built-in microphones, and more. Prepare to spend around $50–$200.

42

GO GREEN WITH SOME PLANTS. A few houseplants will freshen up your space and give you something calming to look at when you're up against a deadline, dealing with an angry client, or preparing for an important presentation. Tailor your plants to your expertise and attentiveness. If you're not a watchful plant parent, don't buy the high-maintenance fiddle-leaf. Instead, go for resilient options that'll thrive even if you forget to water them. For the lowest-maintenance option, consider faux plants. Good ones look so real you'll forget they're not after a week or two.

43

PURCHASE A HEADSET FOR HIGH-QUALITY AUDIO.
You can use your computer's built-in microphone or your
cell phone, of course, but if you're taking more than two calls
a week, buy a headset. Your voice will come across far more
clearly, which your coworkers will appreciate—plus, many
headsets will automatically get rid of any background noise.
If you're typing, the other people on the call won't hear the
clack-clack-clack of your keys. And your experience will
be better too; laptop speaker sounds are usually grainy
and distorted.

44

TUCK YOUR POWER STRIP INTO A CABLE BOX. It's as
simple as opening the lid, inserting your power strip, feeding
the cord out of the slot on both sides of the box, and clos-
ing the lid again. Now all of your unsightly cords are hidden
from sight. You can even mount your cable box underneath
your desk for maximum camouflage. Just remember that it'll
be hard to plug and unplug devices into your power strip or
surge protector if it's boxed up, so this might not be the hack
for you if you're always taking out your charger or inserting
random cords.

45

ADD ART FOR A FINISHING TOUCH. Pick one eye-catching piece to serve as the focal point, group several complementary pieces together to form a vignette, or create a gallery wall with several framed prints of different sizes. Framing your art makes your space look more polished than tacking some old posters to the wall. You'll also appreciate the eye candy when your energy is flagging. Just remember your coworkers, clients, and boss will probably end up seeing this art during a video call, so save anything that's not PG for a different room.

46

USE VIRTUAL BACKGROUNDS. If your workplace is a little less formal, take a background for a spin. Not only will you lighten the mood of your call, but you can also literally camouflage anything in the background you don't want people seeing (like your unmade bed). Most web-conferencing platforms, including Zoom and Webex, have a few preset backgrounds—as well as the option of uploading your own. If you have a professional webcam, it might come with virtual backgrounds too. Try a picture from your company's headquarters (your coworkers will do a double take), a conference room, or a beautiful nature scene.

47

USE A PORTABLE GREEN SCREEN TO COMBAT PATCHY VIRTUAL BACKGROUNDS. Virtual backgrounds work best with solid-colored backgrounds, like a wall with nothing on it. However, if you're *not* in front of a blank wall, put up a portable green screen. Choose a lightweight version you can bring wherever you go, which will be especially helpful for working while you travel.

48

DIY YOUR OWN GREEN SCREEN WITH AN EXTRA SHEET. This is a great hack when you're working on the road but still need a virtual background for your video calls. If you're staying at a hotel, ask the front desk for an extra sheet; if you're at an Airbnb, use the sheets from your bed or ask your host if there are extras in the linen closet. Choose linen or cotton over silk or percale if you can; the shinier the sheet, the more reflective it is. Hanging the sheet up is probably the hardest part. Try Command hooks, which won't cause any damage to the wall, a clothesline and clothespins, or even draping the sheet over a large piece of furniture.

49

AVOID "BLOOPERS" WITH A WEBCAM COVER. This inexpensive gadget sits over your laptop camera. When you're on a video call, you pull the tab to uncover the camera; when you're not on a call, you slide the tab back into place to cover the camera. Using a cover means that even if you accidentally turn your camera on while you're, say, joining a meeting from bed or in less-than-professional attire, your coworkers won't have a clue. (They won't know you're using a cover: They'll just see a blank screen.)

50

PUT A PEN AND NOTEPAD AT YOUR DESK TO TAKE NOTES ON THE FLY. When you need to jot down a random thought or action item during a meeting, your supplies will be at hand. Writing a physical note is a lot less distracting for the other participants than pulling up a virtual notepad and typing—especially if you're mid-presentation.

51

SKIP THE PRINTER. Thanks to e-signature tools that let you sign documents online and phone cameras that are even better than scanners, you might not need a printer. Work for a month without one and see how many times you need to print or scan. (You can always print at your local library or UPS branch in a pinch!)

52

DON'T FORGET ABOUT YOUR BACKDROP. What do an unmade bed, an overflowing clothes hamper, and a questionable poster have in common? When they're behind you on a video call, they'll distract your coworkers and make you look less professional. Make sure you clean up before you start any meetings—or avoid the issue entirely by positioning yourself in front of a wall.

53

RECONSIDER THE SHREDDER. Shredders are useful if your role involves sensitive and/or financial paperwork. However, now that so many documents are kept in the cloud, you might not need one in your home office. Unless you relied on a shredder before you went remote, or your manager recommends you get one, try working without one before you make the call.

54

KEEP DRINKS AND SNACKS IN A MINI FRIDGE. An essential, this is not. But if you want to avoid running to the kitchen fridge all day long, buying a personal fridge and keeping it near the desk will do the trick. Stock it with water and healthy snacks to encourage yourself to make good choices.

55

MAKE SURE YOUR WI-FI IS UP TO THE TASK. It doesn't matter what job you have: You're going to need to connect to the Internet. The strength of the connection you'll need, however, depends on what you're doing. For answering emails and other lightweight tasks, 2–5 megabits per second (Mbps) will suffice. If you're joining video meetings, 5 Mbps is the bare minimum—and you're going to have issues on calls with two-plus participants. For streaming video, sending large files, and other high-bandwidth tasks, 35 Mbps is your target. Do a few online speed tests to see where your connection falls on these spectrums (Fast.com from *Netflix*, and https://projectstream .google.com/speedtest from Google and Measurement Lab are both good options). You might need to consider an upgrade.

56

PLUG YOUR DEVICES INTO A SURGE PROTECTOR. Surge protectors look like power strips, but they're actually more useful. Along with powering multiple devices from a single outlet, a surge protector diverts electricity surges from flooding your electronics and destroying them. It's especially important for gear that uses a lot of power or would be pricey to replace—think your computer, AC unit, stereo, and so on.

57

DON'T FORGET YOUR VIRTUAL TOOL KIT. Many remote workers use their personal computers for work. If that's the case for you, don't forget you'll likely have to install some software. That might be Microsoft Word, Excel, and Power-Point, or more specialized programs for your role, like a CRM for salespeople or accounting software for finance employees. No matter which programs you use, don't wait until you need them to buy and download them.

58

USE A SCREEN AND WEBCAM RECORDING TOOL TO QUICKLY SEND SCREENSHOTS AND VIDEOS. Now that you're working from home, you can't walk over to someone's desk for a quick conversation. Free apps like Loom, Vidyard, and CloudApp fill this gap. Need to show your coworker what you're looking at? Quickly take a screenshot and annotate it with text or arrows. Want to give an update that's too long or nuanced to type out? Record a video. You can even share your screen *and* record yourself at the same time, which is handy when you're walking someone through a slide deck, mock-ups, code, or any other visual document.

5 WAYS TO MOVE YOUR OFFICE OUTSIDE

Many people fantasize about working remotely from a beach. Blue sky overhead, cool drink in hand, water in front of you, sand at your feet...it doesn't get much dreamier than that. Even if you're nowhere near the shore, you can set up a lovely outdoor "office." All you need is a place to sit—your backyard, a balcony, or a quiet park—and these five tips.

59

GO PORTABLE. If you're on your own property, you can probably use your home Wi-Fi. But if you're traveling off the grid, consider buying a Wi-Fi hotspot. This will also be a handy investment if there's an issue with your home Wi-Fi or you need to get a bit of work done while traveling. Similarly, a portable laptop charger will keep your battery (and spirits!) high.

60

TRY OUT A CAMPING CHAIR. If you're considering working outside for just one afternoon, you can bring one of your kitchen chairs outside. But if you're planning to make the "outdoor office" a regular thing or you want the flexibility to change locations easily, go for a camping chair. Look for a lightweight, foldable chair you can sling over your back and will keep you comfortable for hours.

61

DIY A LAPTOP DESK. Trying to balance your laptop, paper-work, phone, and any other items you might need on your lap won't work. Instead, go for a laptop desk, which will slot over your lap or chair arms, depending on its width, and keep your laptop steady while you work. You can purchase one that fits your needs or DIY your own version with a lightweight piece of wood in the proper size.

62

CUT BACK THE GLARE. An anti-glare screen cover is the perfect solution for working outside on a sunny day. Put one of these over your laptop screen to cut down on the sun's glare and let you see during even the brightest time of day.

63

PROTECT YOUR PRIVACY WITH A LAPTOP HOOD. Not only will it protect against glare; a laptop hood will also give you some privacy—so you can answer emails or open sensitive documents in public without worrying who's reading over your shoulder.

· · ·

64

DON'T PUT YOUR ROUTER IN A CORNER. While tucking your router into a media console or closet might be good for aesthetics, it's horrible for your connection. For the strongest Wi-Fi, put your router out in the open and as close to your workspace as possible.

65

MAKE SURE YOUR GEAR ISN'T OUT OF DATE. Router technology evolves pretty quickly—it's recommended you upgrade every three or four years. If you know your router has been around for longer than six, get a new one.

66

AUTOMATE YOUR ROUTER REBOOTS. This hack is essential if your household is using ten or more devices at once. Between your phones, computers, voice assistant devices, smart lights, smart security systems, smart TV, smart refrigerator, smart thermostat, and more, the number of requests you're putting on your router can quickly overwhelm it. Rebooting your router each night will help keep those requests manageable. Get an appliance timer ($10–$20) or a smart plug ($15–$45), plug your router in, and set up your reboot schedule.

67

PLUG IN AN ETHERNET CABLE FOR SUPER RELIABLE INTERNET. Most people can get along just fine with Wi-Fi. However, if your Internet is dropping on a regular basis, get an Ethernet cable. Ethernet is less convenient than Wi-Fi—after all, you're tethered to it—but it's far steadier.

68

BOOST YOUR SIGNAL. A basement, attic, or backyard office could cause you lots of connection headaches, since you're typically far away from the router. A Wi-Fi extender can save the day by expanding the range of your signal. It acts as another node for your router, connecting to your original Wi-Fi signal and then broadcasting its own. Pick a spot for your extender—ideally where you'll be working—plug it in, and pair it with your Wi-Fi network. You can buy a solid Wi-Fi extender for $20–$30.

69

PIN UP IMPORTANT DOCUMENTS OR NOTES ON A BULLETIN BOARD. You'll keep your desk or worktable free of loose papers *and* make them easily visible. A corkboard is also a handy place to hang up inspiration, such as pictures, quotes, or letters.

70

BRAINSTORM WITH A WHITEBOARD. Most office conference rooms have whiteboards for scribbling down ideas, explaining visual concepts, and taking notes. Replicate this experience in your home office with a dry-erase board. Mount it to the wall to preserve space, or get one you can wheel around for maximum flexibility. If you want to brainstorm with your colleagues, make sure the board can be positioned in front of the webcam.

71

SEE IF YOUR COMPANY WILL PAY FOR SOME (OR ALL) OF YOUR WORK-FROM-HOME SETUP. Because you're not contributing to traditional business expenses, like office space; cleaning, maintenance, and security; and tech and equipment; many employers will subsidize the costs of working remotely. Ask if you are eligible for a flat stipend—such as $1,500 a year to be used on WFH expenses—or if you can submit specific purchases for reimbursement. In most cases, your company will pay for your computer and any necessary software. Some companies will also cover a desk and chair, Internet, and a second monitor. If you're lucky, you may get a budget for a coworking space or networking coffees.

72

LOOK FOR TAX DEDUCTIONS. Working from home for yourself? You could be eligible for the home office deduction. If you use part of your home solely for doing business—in other words, you don't use that space for anything other than work—*and* it's the primary place you work, good news. You might be able to write off some of your rent/mortgage, insurance, repairs, utilities, security, and so on. Check with a certified tax advisor to make sure you qualify.

73

PACK A "WORK-ON-THE-GO" BAG. A well-equipped home office is great, but occasionally you're bound to miss having other people around. To ward off feelings of loneliness, try getting outside your home. Keep a bag packed with essential work materials like a computer charger, a phone charger, and headphones so you can simply slip in your laptop and go. Try working from a coffee shop, visiting a coworking space (or asking a friend if you can be their plus-one), or grabbing a carrel at the local library. You can even take turns working from the homes of other remote workers who live near you. Since your stuff will already be packed, you can leave the house without worrying if you forgot anything.

74

MAKE "LOCATION" YOUR NUMBER ONE PRIORITY FOR COWORKING SPACES. Signing up for a shared office space can be a fantastic way to get the benefits of in-person work—like networking, a dedicated place to work, socializing opportunities, and more—with the benefits of working from home. Prioritize proximity over all other factors. After all, the coworking space across town with the impressive décor and weekly happy hours might sound more appealing than the humbler one a few blocks away, but which will you actually get more use of? The place you can get to in ten minutes.

CHAPTER 2

BUILDING ROUTINES AND SCHEDULES

75

CREATE A NEW COMMUTE. Getting to skip the commute is one of the best parts of working from home. However, it also means the lines between "work" and "home" get blurry. To help your brain recognize you're shifting modes, take a walk or bike ride before you start work and again when you log off. You can even go for a quick drive, if that's what feels normal to you.

76

LINE UP MEETINGS IN A ROW. Jumping from a meeting to independent work and back into a meeting eats up a huge amount of your mental energy, thanks to the "context switching" brain tax. If possible, try to cluster your calls. This lets you knock out all of your (virtual) face time at once—then you can tackle work that requires deeper focus.

77

TAKE THE SAME ROUTE OR LISTEN TO THE SAME THING EVERY TIME YOU TAKE YOUR COMMUTE. This gives your brain an additional mental cue that your workday is about to begin or end. To make your commute something you look forward to, use it to pick up coffee or breakfast at a local spot or a snack at the end of the day. For a nonedible treat, listen to your favorite podcast.

78

SET—AND STICK TO—A SCHEDULE. The schedule itself doesn't matter, as long as it's compatible with your work, team's expectations, and lifestyle. Sticking to the schedule *does* matter. Maybe you get up each morning at 6 a.m., work on solo projects for two hours, have meetings until noon, eat lunch with your kids, and then answer emails for another hour before you call it a day. Or maybe you get up at 10 a.m., have a quick breakfast, and work until 7 p.m. Having a consistent routine will help you stay productive without overdoing it.

79

WAKE UP AT THE SAME TIME EVERY MORNING. Without the built-in expectation of arriving at the office by a specific hour, you might find yourself lingering in bed later and later. Not only does a delayed wake-up start the day off on an unproductive note; it means you'll head to bed later than usual too. That's bad for your productivity and sense of routine. To give your workweek structure and consistency, make an effort to get out of bed at a regular time each morning.

80

ALWAYS MAKE YOUR BED. Whether you work from home or in the office, this routine will make you feel calmer and more collected. And even though it takes just five minutes, it'll give you a sense of accomplishment—which means you'll be in a good mindset for starting the day. Making the bed is especially important for remote employees, since you'll probably be walking in and out of your bedroom all day. A tidy bed makes the entire physical *and* mental space feel less messy.

81

BEGIN THE DAY PEACEFULLY WITH A NATURAL LIGHT ALARM CLOCK. If you hate the piercing wail of a traditional alarm, try a light therapy (or "sunrise") version. These clocks rely on light, not sound, to wake you up, slowly getting brighter and brighter to mimic the gradual brightening of the sun. It doesn't matter how dark it is outside; your room will be bathed in light, telling your body it's time to get up. You'll easily transition from sleep to wakefulness and feel more alert and well rested once you do.

82

WAKE UP DURING YOUR LIGHTEST SLEEP PHASE. It's a lot easier to spring out of bed when you're awoken during stage one to two of sleep (light) versus stages three to four (deep) or five (REM). Apps like Sleep Cycle and SleepScore let you set your target wake-up window (such as 6–7 a.m.), then use your iPhone or Android to identify when you're in the right sleep stage to wake up. These tools come with detailed sleep reports as well so you can learn which lifestyle factors lead to your most restful nights.

83

IGNORE THE MYTH OF THE EARLY BIRD. Most of us have the same number of productive hours in the day no matter when we start and stop working. Now that you work remotely, you don't need to force yourself into being a morning person if you're actually a night owl. Spend a week documenting the times you wake up sans alarm. If you *do* have to set an alarm for a meeting or errand, pay attention to how you feel that day. Are you groggier than normal? Or do you feel fine? At the end of the week, use your notes to figure out your optimal sleep schedule. Then adjust your work hours accordingly. (Just make sure your manager signs off on these: You might need to be online for a specific time.)

84

SET YOUR CORE HOURS. Unless all of your communication with your coworkers and boss can take place asynchronously—on separate timelines—there are fixed hours you'll need to be online each day. In a traditional workplace, these hours are roughly the same for everyone: 8 or 9 a.m. until 5 or 6 p.m. However, as a remote worker, your core hours can shift. Say you're most productive in the evening: Your core hours might be 11 a.m. to 7 p.m. Work with your manager, peers, and any people you manage to set the times you should be available for instant messages and meetings each day. If your team works across several time zones, prioritize the hours when everyone overlaps.

85

GIVE THE "FLEX SCHEDULE" A GO. Once you know when you need to be online (and you've gotten the green light from your boss), try flexible working. Any schedule that deviates from the standard Monday through Friday 9 a.m. to 5 p.m. is considered flexible. Do you need to get your kids ready for school in the morning and pick them up in the afternoon? Try working from 5 a.m. to 7 a.m., going offline until 8:30 a.m., and then wrapping up your day at 3:30 p.m. Or perhaps you volunteer every Friday, so you work a half day then and a half day on Saturday. Aim to fit your schedule to your life, not the other way around.

86

USE TIME BOXING TO MANAGE AN OVERWHELMING TO-DO LIST. Take time blocking (i.e., scheduling blocks of time throughout the day for specific activities) and to-do lists, put them together, and you get time boxing. This time management technique calls for giving each task a deadline. For instance, you might commit to writing all of your reports' performance reviews between 10 a.m. and noon, writing your own self-evaluation from 1 to 1:45 p.m., and finalizing your team retreat agenda from 2 to 3 p.m. Time boxing is a good fit if you struggle with procrastination or unrealistic to-do lists. Make this a part of your morning routine; if you map out your plan for the day first thing, you'll have a better idea of what you should accomplish and where you have flexibility in your schedule.

87

COMBAT MUSCLE FATIGUE AND TAKE A BREAK AT THE SAME TIME BY STRETCHING. You can use your work breaks to stretch, which will give you an energy boost and help alleviate any soreness from sitting at a desk all day. Stretch Reminder is an iPhone and Android app designed specifically for people who sit a lot. It asks you when you'd like to be reminded to stretch and which body parts you want to focus on. Each reminder comes with an easy-to-follow video walking you through the stretch.

88

GIVE EACH DAY A THEME. This routine eliminates context switching and is ideal for creatures of habit or anyone with a highly predictable workload. Here's how it works: Each day of the week has a separate focus. Maybe Monday is for creating social media content, Tuesday is for checking in with clients, Wednesday is for analyzing content performance, Thursday is for crafting presentations, and Friday is for miscellaneous tasks. Day theming can require some juggling (for example, perhaps some clients don't want to meet on Tuesday, or you need to have a presentation ready before Thursday). But if you can make it work, it'll allow you to delve deeply into each task type.

89

TAKE REGULAR BREAKS. Without coworkers to chat with, a cafeteria or kitchen to walk to, and, of course, the commute, remote workers might find themselves taking far fewer breaks than office workers. Don't let yourself fall into this habit; breaks are essential for your mental health and quality of work. If you're typically in meetings all day, schedule five- to fifteen-minute breaks every few hours on your calendar. And if your work is more independent, set timers on your phone reminding you to get up from your desk for a bit.

90

TRY THE POMODORO TECHNIQUE. There's a reason this time management strategy is so popular: It works! The concept is simple. You pick a task, then set a timer for twenty-five minutes. Don't move on from that task until you're done—if you get distracted by another thought, write it down on a piece of paper. When the timer buzzes, take a quick four-minute break before getting back to work. After four "Pomodoros," take a twenty- to thirty-minute break. If you struggle to stay motivated (especially for longer periods of time) and need a straightforward system, the Pomodoro Technique might be perfect.

91

FORCE YOURSELF TO TAKE A BREAK. Struggling to actually take breaks? There's an app for that. Stretchly is a free tool that pops up on your screen at preset intervals and tells you to take a breather. By default, you get twenty-second breaks every ten minutes and five-minute breaks every half hour. However, you can customize your break frequency and length. (For instance, if you're following the Pomodoro Technique, you could enable four-minute breaks after every twenty-five-minute work block.) To force yourself to follow through on breaks, turn on "strict mode": This feature means you can't skip a break, postpone it, or finish it early.

92

SCHEDULE YOUR HARDEST TASKS WHEN YOU HAVE THE MOST ENERGY. The "eat the frog" strategy prescribes doing your most difficult project first thing so you can get it out of the way and build the momentum to tackle your remaining to-dos. This technique works if you're a morning person—but if you're not, it makes no sense to tackle your toughest to-do when your energy is lowest. Schedule your "frog" task for your most productive time of day, whether that's the morning, afternoon, or evening.

93

DON'T OPEN YOUR EMAIL OR CHAT UNTIL YOU'RE READY TO WORK. This is especially important if you've got coworkers in different time zones. The team members who have been up for hours will have filled your inbox and company chat channels with messages. If you try to casually skim through these, you'll inevitably get pulled into work mode. Preserve your morning, and avoid the temptation to check Gmail or Slack until you sit down to your computer. (You'll also retain more of what you read when you're not eating breakfast or bleary with sleep.)

94

KEEP BUFFER TIME IN YOUR SCHEDULE TO ACCOMMODATE LAST-MINUTE CHANGES. While it's tempting to schedule every minute of your workday, you'll have no margin for error. Leaving a few slots open will help you readjust on the fly if, for example, you get an urgent question from your boss, a project takes longer than you anticipated, or your meeting runs over.

95

LET YOUR COWORKERS KNOW WHICH EVENTS THEY CAN BOOK OVER. You can either note this in the event title (for example, "Debugging [open for meetings]") or the description ("Holding this block for debugging, but feel free to schedule over this if you can't find another time!"). Just make sure your teammates know the drill. (This hack doesn't work if people can only see when you're available versus individual events, so check if your calendar details are visible first.)

96

EXPERIMENT WITH DIFFERENT ROUTINES. One size does not fit all, so try out a few routines before committing. You never know what might resonate.

HOW TO BOOST YOUR MORNING ROUTINE

Now that you don't have to sit in heavy traffic, bike across town, get on a train or bus, walk to the office—or any combination of those—you have a lot more time to spend on your morning routine. Use these ideas to inspire you...and have a great start to your day.

97

SHAKE OFF YOUR SLEEPINESS WITH A COLD SHOWER. Standing under an ice-cold stream of water might not be the most *pleasant* morning routine, but it'll wake you right up. Cold water speeds up your heart rate and deepens your breathing—giving you a jolt of energy more effective than a cup of coffee.

98

PREPARE COLD BREW THE NIGHT BEFORE. Not only is homemade cold brew easy to prepare with a cold brew coffee maker, but it also makes for an effective nighttime routine. When you wake up the next day, you'll have an entire carafe of chilled coffee waiting for you.

99

PROGRAM YOUR COFFEE MAKER TO BREW COFFEE AT THE PERFECT TIME EVERY MORNING. If you prefer hot coffee, buy a coffee machine with a timer. Set it to begin twenty minutes or so before your workday begins. This hack will help you get on a consistent schedule and take some of the hassle out of your morning. Plus you'll have something to look forward to the minute you get out of bed.

100

GET SOME VITAMIN D. Sunlight tells your body it's time to wake up, which will make that transition out of sleep mode into work mode a lot less painful. Right after your eyes open, part your curtains, raise your blinds, or open your shutters. If your room doesn't get enough natural light in the morning, go outside for a few minutes.

101

MITIGATE ANXIETY WITH A BRAIN DUMP. If you often feel like your thoughts are pulling you in a thousand different directions, try spending ten to fifteen minutes per day writing down everything that's on your mind. Once you've gotten something on paper, it's usually easier to move on. You'll start your workday feeling a little calmer.

102

MULTITASK YOUR MEDITATION. Yes, meditating while you do something else sounds like an oxymoron...but it works! The key? Picking an activity that requires almost zero thought, like taking a walk, brushing your teeth, even waiting for the microwave to finish reheating your food. Find a one- or two-minute meditation you like and start weaving it into your morning or evening routine.

103

COORDINATE A HOUSEHOLD BATHROOM SCHEDULE. Whether you live with roommates, your family, or your partner, coming up with a plan for the bathroom will help you avoid conflict. Sit down with everyone you live with and figure out when each person should shower based on their schedule and how long they need. (Because you work from home, they might assume you can go last—but this isn't necessarily the case depending on your typical meeting schedule.)

104

GIVE YOUR MIND A WARM-UP BEFORE YOU JUMP INTO THE WORKDAY. Read a book, do the crossword, play Sudoku, practice a foreign language, take an online course, or listen to a stimulating podcast. These activities are good halfway points between relaxing and working so you'll feel ready for whatever's on your work agenda.

105

EAT THE SAME BREAKFAST EVERY DAY. It's one less choice you need to make—freeing up mental energy for tougher decisions. If you appreciate the simplicity of this hack but need some culinary novelty, try using a template for your meal and switching up the execution. For instance, you might have toast every morning with different spreads, or oatmeal with a rotation of toppings.

106

PREP FOR YOUR MORNING ROUTINE AT NIGHT. You'll take all the friction out of the process the next morning, which makes you likelier to follow through. Let's say you want to start writing in the mornings. Lay out your journal and pen so they're one of the first things you see when you wake up. This hack can mean the difference between a routine that sticks and one that does not.

. . .

107

BEGIN THE WORKDAY BY SAYING HI TO YOUR TEAM. In the office, you don't have to think about greeting your coworkers every morning—it happens naturally. When you're working from home, you'll need to re-create this routine virtually. Typing "Good morning, how's everyone doing?" takes just a second but helps your team feel connected.

108

CLOCK IN WITH YOUR REMOTE COMMUNITY. If you work for yourself—or simply want to meet other remote workers—you can start the day by checking into a community like *We Work Remotely*, *Workfrom*, and *Remotely One*. The folks in these groups can relate to your work life struggles, give you advice, share their experiences, and even help you win clients. Even though you're sitting at home, you'll feel just as connected to the outside world as you did in a traditional office...maybe even more. Make it part of your routine to check in with these groups regularly.

109

DON'T FIGHT YOUR SLUMP. In the office, you have to push through your low-energy periods. That's not the case when working from home. Take a twenty-minute nap in the afternoon, when you always struggle to tick off even the most basic items from your to-do list. Or do a yoga routine at 11 a.m. when your first cup of coffee has worn off and you need a quick breather. To know when you're at your daily "low point"—or simply unmotivated—use a time-tracking app or WFH log. Looking at your work patterns over time will help you identify the time of day your slump typically occurs.

110

HAVE LOG-ON AND LOG-OFF ROUTINES. Use one routine to kick your day into gear and another to wind it down. You'll start to associate these routines with shifting in and out of work mode. For instance, perhaps your morning routine is making coffee and going for a walk around the neighborhood, while your evening routine is brewing herbal tea and tidying your workspace for tomorrow.

111

KEEP A WORK-FROM-HOME LOG. When you first start working from home, jot down a few quick lines at the end of your workday for a week or two so you can spot trends in your personal WFH productivity and engagement levels. For example, maybe you always get distracted around 3 p.m. when your roommates come home, or do your best work in the early morning when the house is quiet. These notes will help you craft the optimal work routine.

112

PUT ON SHOES BEFORE YOU SIT DOWN TO YOUR COMPUTER. It might sound weird, but wearing a real pair of shoes (read: not slippers) is a reliable way to tell your brain that your workday has begun. If you're worried about tracking dirt inside your home, consider purchasing a pair of shoes you only wear inside. You can even keep these shoes in a basket by your desk or outside your office.

113

NEVER WORK STRAIGHT UP TO YOUR BEDTIME. Just like you need a buffer in the morning, you need a buffer between working and getting into bed at night. (This is usually an issue for people who get more energy as the day goes on, since their highest-productivity time is later.) If you do find yourself burning the midnight oil, make sure you spend at least an hour winding down. Close your laptop, put on pajamas, brush your teeth, read a book—you'll feel much calmer by the time you drift into sleep.

114

DON'T SKIP THE SHOWER. Your coworkers can't smell you over Skype, so, technically, you can get away with not showering. That being said, skipping the shower isn't recommended. Showering does two things: It tells your brain you're getting ready for the day, and it requires you to change your clothes. Feeling presentable and prepared is an important part of showing up to work—even if you're showing up on a webcam, not in an office.

HACK YOUR CLOSET FOR PROFESSIONAL (YET COMFY!) WORK-FROM-HOME WEAR

Freedom from the shackles of corporate dress codes is a major perk of working remotely. That being said, it's hard to take yourself seriously when you're rocking pajamas or sweatpants—which will affect your focus and motivation, not to mention confidence in meetings. In addition, if there's no distinction between what you wear to bed and what you wear to work, the line between life and work will quickly dissolve. Add changing from your relaxed clothes into "professional" ones to your WFH morning routine to combat these effects. When you're logging out for the night, do another outfit change. These pieces will keep you comfortable yet presentable—the best of both worlds.

115

CHOOSE STRETCH DENIM. Stay comfy *and* professional with stretch denim. You'll get the structure of jeans with the forgiving stretch of leggings. And if someone rings your doorbell mid-meeting, your coworkers won't get an eyeful of your decade-old sweatpants when you get up to answer it.

116

WEAR LINEN WHEN IT'S HOT. Your office probably has air-conditioning...but your home might not. To look professional while avoiding overheating, choose a top, dress, or shorts made of linen. This easy, breathable fabric will keep you cool in even the most sweltering temps.

117

PUT ON A SILK BUTTON-DOWN FOR FANCY OCCASIONS. When you're meeting with your CEO, VIP client, or potential employer, this is a great option. Silk button-downs look classy and are light, airy, and comfortable.

118

LOOK GREAT ON VIDEO WITH COTTON T-SHIRTS. Work in a pretty casual environment? You can never go wrong with a simple cotton T-shirt. Just make sure whatever prints, patterns, and logos you choose are work-appropriate.

119

SWAP BLANKET WRAPS FOR SWEATERS. In the chilly months, opt for pullovers or sweaters, which will give you more warmth and heft. You'll look much more professional than if you were cocooned in your favorite blanket—your coworkers might even think you were napping instead of working!

120

GET READY QUICKLY WITH CARDIGANS. Last-minute meeting got you rushing? A well-fitting cardigan takes two seconds to put on but implies you made an effort.

121

GET EXTRA FLEXIBILITY WITH COMMUTER PANTS. These pants, typically made from a water-repellent, elastic material, are along for the ride whether you're sitting at your desk, biking to a coffee shop, or taking a midday walk break. If your WFH schedule is a bit more active, these are the pants for you.

122

SELECT COMFORTABLE (BUT SUPPORTIVE) SHOES. These shoes are made for...standing? Fortunately for your feet, there's no need to wear dress shoes when you're working from home. If you're alternating between sitting and standing, pick footwear that'll transition with you. That might mean a well-fitting pair of sneakers, comfortable flats, socks, or even bare feet. Test out a range of options and see what you like best.

123

FILTER OUT BLUE LIGHT WITH SPECIAL GLASSES. These days, you can have twenty-twenty vision and still wear specs. Blue light glasses block out the artificial blue light that beams out of computers, phones, tablets, and other screens. Some options even help reduce glare. Many people who wear blue light glasses say their eyes are no longer strained by long days of staring at their laptop; they also report better sleep. (That being said, the jury is still out on the medical benefits of blue light glasses. If your eyesight or sleep is suffering, the most important step you can take is reducing your total screen time.)

· · ·

124

GET TWO HOURS OF OUTDOORS TIME A WEEK. According to a 2019 study published in *Scientific Reports*, people who spend two-plus hours in nature each week are healthier and have higher levels of well-being. The researchers say it doesn't make a difference how you get in those 120 minutes. You can take one extra-long walk on the weekend or seven twenty-minute walks every day. (And more time isn't necessarily better; the benefits level out at 200–300 minutes.) With this in mind, try tracking your nature time each week and making an effort to clear two hours.

125

TURN OFF THE CAMERA ON PAJAMA-FRIENDLY DAYS.
Some days it happens—all your routines fly out the window and you never get out of your pajamas. If you flout the rules and wear pajamas to a meeting, keep your camera off. Need to make an on-screen appearance? Swap out your cozy top for a "professional" one and make sure you don't stand up while in the meeting. Revealing some less-professional bottoms is one of the cardinal WFH mistakes. Avoid it.

126

FINISH THE DAY BY WRITING OUT YOUR PRIORITIES FOR THE NEXT. That way, when you sit down at your desk the next morning, you'll have a clear sense of what you need to accomplish. This helps you get focused immediately— instead of wasting valuable time trying to remember what you'd been working on the day before. Try to keep your list of priorities reasonable: If you write down too many, you'll feel overwhelmed.

127

LAY OUT YOUR CLOTHES THE NIGHT BEFORE. It might seem silly; after all, your closet isn't going anywhere, and neither are you. But picking out the next day's outfit means you're likelier to actually change. This is a good routine to establish if you find yourself staying in your pajamas for most or all of the workday.

128

HAVE A STANDING CALL WITH A FRIEND OR FAMILY MEMBER. It's common for remote workers to struggle with social isolation. To combat this, schedule a weekly call with someone you feel close to, whether that's a friend, mentor, or loved one. Having this conversation at the same time every week will let you plan other obligations around it, meaning you're likelier to follow through even when life gets hectic (and that's often when you need this the most!).

129

BUILD YOUR SCHEDULE AROUND YOUR DAILY WORK LOCATION. If you're a creature of habit, your routine might be to set up shop in the same part of your house every day. But if you crave constant variety, vary locations throughout the week. Establishing a "pattern" of locations will help you figure out a routine. For example, you might work from your friend's coworking space on Mondays, which lets you network and brainstorm with others. You might schedule your deep work for Tuesdays and Wednesdays when you work in the library. If you're at home on most Thursdays and Fridays, you already know the best time to schedule your meetings, calls, and presentations. Switching up your location will keep boredom at bay and gives you something to look forward to...while still allowing you to build a schedule that suits your tasks.

130

HAVE A FITNESS ROUTINE. You've probably noticed exercise makes you feel better. Moving your body has incredible positive effects, from lowering anxiety and boosting your mood to increasing your productivity and motivation. Since you work from home, you have more opportunities to get a workout in than many people. Take advantage of it! Create a fitness routine that fits into your day—whether that's going for a run in the morning, lifting weights at lunch, doing yoga in the afternoon, or taking a salsa class at night.

131

END THE WEEK BY PREPARING FOR THE UPCOMING ONE. Beat the Sunday Scaries and set up your future self for success. This routine lets you fully enjoy your weekend without getting stressed by the week ahead. First, look at your planned meetings. Figure out what prework, if any, you need to do for those—whether that's pulling together everything you'd like to discuss with your manager in your one-on-one or practicing your slides for team training. Next, schedule any focus work you'd like to get done. Getting this time in your calendar early will ensure it won't get sucked up by last-minute requests or meetings. Finally, review your personal obligations (including errands, housework, social plans, etc.). Make sure you've got adequate time for all these too.

132

EMBRACE THE POWER NAP. Yes, you read that correctly. Napping for fifteen to twenty minutes is an excellent way to recharge. After your nap, you'll experience a burst of energy—like you've just had a cup of coffee, but without the jitteriness. Naps can also help you catch up on sleep if you didn't get enough the night before and even boost your mood and memory. Just make sure you set an alarm: If you sleep for *too* long, you'll actually feel groggier than you were pre-nap. You should also avoid taking a nap too close to your bedtime (for most people, that's after 3 p.m.).

133

DON'T BEAT YOURSELF UP IF YOU HAVE TO BREAK FROM ROUTINE. Routines are important: They ground you, give you a sense of comfort and control, and help you work more effectively. That being said, don't get so attached to your routine that you can't pivot. If you need to jump on an emergency meeting during your deep work block, that's okay. Take the meeting, then give yourself a few minutes to shift back into focus mode and continue with your day. Routines should work for you—not the other way around.

134

BUILD REWARDS INTO YOUR ROUTINE. If you're using time boxing, time batching, or another time-based productivity routine, give yourself a reward each time you finish a work block. If you're operating by a to-do list, give yourself a reward every set number of tasks you finish. Change up the rewards throughout the day; for instance, your morning reward might be scrolling through *Instagram* for ten minutes, while your evening reward is a beer. You can even add your rewards to your calendar or to-do list to give yourself visual motivation.

135

SHARE YOUR ROUTINE WITH THE PEOPLE YOU LIVE WITH. The more insight into your daily work patterns they have, the more support or flexibility they can give you. Suppose your morning routine includes meditating for twenty minutes. If your roommate or partner knows your plan, they won't knock on your door when it's closed. And make an effort to accommodate their routines as well. Do they like to cook a big breakfast around 8 a.m. each morning? Once you know that, you can take early calls in the living room instead of at the kitchen table.

136

SCHEDULE OFFICE VISITS EVERY FIVE TO TEN BUSI-NESS DAYS. This hack only applies if you live within an hour of the office. If you can swing it, this routine actually gives you the best of both worlds: face time combined with the flexibility of a WFH lifestyle. It's especially important to occasionally work from the office if you're the only remote person on your team—if you're not intentional about seeing your coworkers regularly, you'll probably miss out on important conversations and seem less "visible."

137

DO A CAREER CHECK-IN EVERY QUARTER. According to a 2014 study from Stanford University economist Nicholas A. Bloom, remote workers might be 50 percent less likely to get promotions than in-office employees. That's not a fun fact to read if you're working from home. To make sure your career growth doesn't stall, evaluate your professional development every three months. Ask yourself, "What have I accomplished since my last check-in? What new skills have I picked up? What new projects have I worked on? Is my manager completely aware of this progress? What am I working toward for the next three months?" This exercise will highlight whether you're making steady traction and promoting your accomplishments.

138

TRAVEL AND WORK AT THE SAME TIME. Unlike traditional employees, who are fixed to a specific location, remote workers can roam the globe. If you love to travel, consider taking a work-travel trip every quarter or year. (Some people, known as digital nomads, travel and work full time.) Working from a brand-new place will inspire and rejuvenate you.

139

ADAPT YOUR WORK ROUTINE FOR TRAVEL. This routine needs to be more flexible than your regular one so it can accommodate a new location, workspace, or time zone. Figure out the core building blocks of your day—such as "eat breakfast," "get to inbox zero," "go for a walk," "meet with the team," and so on—then rearrange those blocks as needed. Your adjusted routine will help you preserve a sense of normalcy even when you're in a different place.

140

ATTEND A CONFERENCE EVERY THREE TO TWELVE MONTHS. Yes, conferences should be part of your routine. Whether you're participating in a virtual or in-person event, you'll get the opportunity to learn from experts, meet others in your field, and discover inspiration and ideas. Try to attend conferences with your coworkers so you can compare notes and, more importantly, strengthen your professional relationship.

141

DO A DIGITAL DETOX EVERY MONTH OR QUARTER.
Back up old files to the cloud and/or a hard drive; archive
emails you don't need anymore; centralize your file system;
clean up all your screenshots, GIFs, and other random media;
and delete any apps or extensions you're no longer using. This
might feel tedious, but you'll free up space on your computer,
declutter your virtual life, and make it easier to surface the
tools and information you need. Set up a calendar reminder to
make sure you do it consistently.

142

**READ THE COMPANY BLOG, WIKI, OR KNOWLEDGE
BASE.** Without in-person chatter, you need to go out of
your way to stay clued in. Make a habit of spending twenty
to sixty minutes each week reading the latest posts on your
company's internal "bulletin board." This ensures you'll always
know what's going on outside your immediate team. (If you're
a freelancer, you should still practice this routine—but swap
"company blog" for "industry websites.")

143

VISIT YOUR COMPANY HEADQUARTERS TWO TO FOUR TIMES A YEAR. Thanks to platforms like Zoom, Skype, and Google Hangouts, virtual face-to-face time is nearly as good as the in-person equivalent. But nothing beats the bonding and brainstorming you can do with your colleagues when you're all in the same room. To ensure you get this essential interaction time, ask your manager if you can travel to HQ every quarter or half year. There might even be a dedicated budget for remote employee travel.

144

PLAN A MONTHLY OR QUARTERLY MEETUP WITH OTHER REMOTE TEAM MEMBERS IN YOUR AREA. Do you live within a hundred miles of other people at your company? See if they're game to get together regularly. This meetup can be purely social, or you can arrange a workday. Rent a workspace, meet at a coffee shop, or go to someone's home, and spend a few hours working remotely together. You'll experience a greater sense of connection to your organization, ward off any feelings of isolation, and get in some valuable networking.

CHAPTER 3

CREATING NEW COMMUNICATION HABITS

145

ASK QUESTIONS INSTEAD OF MAKING STATEMENTS.
Leaping to conclusions doesn't do your relationships any
favors—and as a remote employee with fewer opportunities to
build rapport, one bad interaction can color an entire relationship. Instead of making statements, ask questions. Swap "You
should have done such and such" with "Did you consider doing such and such?" and "That project should already be well
underway" with "Did you have a chance to start that project?"
This approach lets you get additional information without putting your team member or direct report on the defensive.

146

ASSUME BEST INTENT. Without the benefit of someone's
facial expressions, gestures, and voice, it's easy to misinterpret their tone on a chat or in an email. Your coworker might
quickly write "okay" because they're running to a meeting,
but without that context, you might wonder if they're
annoyed at your request. Not so bad when it happens once...
but these miscommunications can quickly add up, which will
impact your work relationships. If you're picking up on nega-
tivity, remind yourself to give people the benefit of the doubt.

147

DON'T BE AFRAID TO ASK FOR CLARITY. Not sure how to interpret someone's message? Just ask what they meant. This is the quickest way to stop a misunderstanding in its tracks. Write something like "I wasn't sure how to read your last message. Can you give me more context/would you mind rephrasing?" Your coworkers will appreciate the effort to understand.

148

HAVE SENSITIVE CONVERSATIONS ON VIDEO CALLS. These talks are already tricky to navigate, so you want to see the other person's face and hear their voice. As soon as a conversation goes into tense or delicate territory, say, "Hey, do you have fifteen minutes to hop on a call? I think it would be easier to chat face-to-face." If you can't meet right then, say, "This seems important, so I'd love to schedule some time to go through it with you. Do you want to meet at X time (tomorrow, this afternoon) to talk?"

149

RESPOND IN AN APPROPRIATE AMOUNT OF TIME.
What's appropriate depends on the platform. When your coworker sends you a message on chat, they'll probably look for a response within a few hours. But when they send you an email, they won't expect an immediate answer. Try to answer chat messages the same day you get them and emails in twenty-four to forty-eight business hours. (Factor in the message's urgency as well; if your coworker sends you an emergency email, you should respond ASAP.)

150

ACKNOWLEDGE THE ORIGINAL MESSAGE. When you receive an email or chat, your response doesn't have to fulfill the request or answer the question—it can simply acknowledge you've read the message. Of course, if the ask is urgent or small, address it right away. But if it's not timely and will take more than a few hours (or even a few days), letting the sender know you're working on their request is an acceptable response. Say, "Thanks for reaching out. I'll look into this and will get back to you by (reasonable date) or sooner."

151

SAVE TIME WITH A TEXT EXPANDER TOOL. Creating templates is a great way to save time while still getting your message across. Software like TextExpander (Mac, Windows, and Chrome) and Alfred (Mac) lets you insert text snippets into whatever you're typing using custom keyboard shortcuts. To save time, create templates for your most-used responses. For example, you might create a "/late" snippet that expands into this message: "Hey there, my meeting is running over, but I'll be there in five."

152

CREATE A "HOW TO WORK WITH ME" GUIDE. This guide will help your coworkers work with you more effectively; plus, the process of writing it might give you some valuable insights into your preferences. You can include anything you think your team members and/or direct reports should know, such as the communication methods you prefer for giving or receiving updates, your optimal meeting times, any scheduling limitations, the best way to give you feedback, and other pertinent information. Aim for one or two pages. You want your manual to be short and sweet so your colleagues can quickly digest it.

153

ENCOURAGE YOUR COWORKERS TO CREATE THEIR OWN "HOW TO WORK WITH ME" GUIDES. Just like there are cheat codes to working most effectively with you, there are cheat codes for your team members and manager. This is one shortcut you should take; knowing your colleagues' individual work preferences will improve your relationships overnight. To make it as easy as possible, share a template they can fill out. And then, most importantly, do your best to follow their preferences and reference their guide often.

154

SCHEDULE DAILY "STAND-UPS." Without random interactions at the coffee machine or conversations at your desks, your coworkers may feel distant. A daily ten-minute "stand-up" when everyone shares what they're working on will keep you in the loop. If your coworkers are on different time zones, making a morning stand-up impossible to schedule, try an asynchronous one: Everyone records a quick video update or writes a three- to four-sentence update in your team channel. You'll feel a bit more connected knowing exactly what everyone is working on that day.

155

DON'T FLOOD YOUR TEAM MEMBERS WITH MESSAGES.
When you're in the office with a quick or urgent question, it might be easiest to walk over to your coworkers' desks to ask them in person. But if you're working remotely, you have to rely on the technology at hand...and your coworkers' willingness to respond in a timely manner. So make sure you're using that technology in the most effective way possible. Few things will stress out (or irritate) your coworkers faster than getting pelted with the same question or notification on text, chat, *and* email. Pick the right medium for the message—which depends on how urgently you need a reply—and send it just once.

156

GIVE PEOPLE A CHANCE TO RESPOND BEFORE YOU SEND A FOLLOW-UP MESSAGE. Like all communication, how long you wait depends on the context. If you sent your coworkers a time-critical question, and they don't respond in an hour, give them a nudge. But if you emailed them yesterday about a low-priority project, wait at least one more day before following up.

157

ADD CONTEXT TO YOUR FIRST MESSAGE. Do you ever start with "Hey, so-and-so, how's it going?"—or, worse, just "Hi"—and wait for a response before getting to your point? Whether you're remote or not, this habit is annoying: It forces your coworker to engage without knowing what you need. (They might even ignore you until you explain!) Not only will your conversation take longer; you'll also ruffle some feathers for no reason. Luckily, there's an easy fix. Explain why you're reaching out in the first or second message, *then* pause for your team member's answer.

158

USE PUBLIC CHANNELS OVER PRIVATE CHANNELS. To promote transparency and trust, have conversations in public chat rooms whenever possible. This also cuts down on confusion and information silos; when a new hire or employee from another department is looking for something, they can search your company's chat instead of bugging you for the info. Only move discussions to private channels when they involve sensitive or confidential information.

159

MAKE IT CLEAR WHAT YOU NEED IN YOUR EMAIL SUBJECT LINE. It might seem obvious what you're looking for and when, but the people you're emailing have less context. Adding a label to your subject line will help them see at a glance if they need to open and respond to your email immediately or if they can give it some time. Not only will you avoid confusion and unnecessary follow-up questions, but you'll get a better response rate. To give you an idea, here are some labels to include in your subject line:

» No response necessary
» Action required
» Please let me know you've read this by X date
» Please take Y action by Z time

160

ASK YOUR BOSS HOW MUCH TRANSPARENCY INTO YOUR SCHEDULE THEY'D LIKE. Some bosses want a heads-up every time you're stepping away from work for more than thirty minutes; others couldn't care less if you're offline for hours, as long as your work gets done and you don't leave your coworkers in the lurch. Not sure where your manager falls on the spectrum? Ask them.

161

RECORD A VIDEO INSTEAD OF SCHEDULING A MEET-ING. Have you noticed your calendar fill up with meetings since you started working from home? You're not alone. Remote employees tend to default to meetings for communicating, since it's the closest replacement for in-person conversations. But it doesn't take long to burn out on meetings. Not to mention, they can be inefficient. For updates, detailed instructions, project overviews, and similar types of communication, try filming an informal video instead. Free recording tools like Loom, CloudApp, and Vidyard make this easy. Try encouraging your coworkers to do the same.

162

USE PRIVATE MESSAGES SPARINGLY. A direct message (or one-to-one communication between two-plus people) should be your last resort. Use these for conversations where an appropriate private channel doesn't exist. Private messages are also ideal for random or nonwork-related discussions your other coworkers won't care about. For example, if you see a funny video that reminds you of a team member, a direct message is likely better than a post in your team channel. (But take your cues from the people above you. If your boss posts funny videos in your team chat, you've got the green light to do so too.)

163

USE YOUR CHAT STATUS TO SET EXPECTATIONS FOR YOUR RESPONSE TIME. If you're going on a midday walk, picking your kids up from school, or running errands, add your activity to your status with an expected return time. Here's an example: "Lunchtime jog—back by 1:30 p.m." This tells your team members when to expect a reply. If you don't feel comfortable sharing what you're doing, simply write when you'll be back online, like so: "Away from my computer until 1:30 p.m."

164

STEP UP YOUR COMMUNICATION CADENCE SO YOU'RE MORE VISIBLE. In a regular office, you're visible by default. When you work from home, you need to go out of your way to gain visibility. *How* you do that depends on the internal culture and communication style. Do most discussions take place over chat? React to and comment on more posts. Is the wiki where everyone goes to share news, project updates, experiments, and so on? Like more pages, leave more responses, and look for opportunities to document your own takeaways. Treat participating in your team's culture and discussions as a part of your job.

165

GIVE YOURSELF VISIBILITY GOALS. "Be more visible" is a vague goal. To make it more attainable, set concrete visibility goals for yourself. To give you an idea, you might commit to attending one online social event per month, having a virtual coffee chat with a coworker twice per month, and sharing an interesting article with your coworkers on chat three times per month. Track your progress in a spreadsheet.

166

KEEP CHANNEL CONVERSATIONS ON TRACK. Chat messages feel more casual than emails or even meetings, so it's easy to forget you're having conversations with your coworkers—not your friends. But bringing up a topic that doesn't belong in that channel will make you look out of touch with professional norms. If you're in a channel dedicated to a new product launch, don't start a discussion of your company's latest office opening. If you're in a channel for diagnosing product issues, don't ask about everyone's weekend plans. When in doubt, read the channel description and pay attention to the topics other people in the channel are (and aren't) discussing.

167

ASK YOUR BOSS FOR FEEDBACK AROUND YOUR VISIBILITY. Next time you're discussing your professional development or remote work experience, say, "I'm working on raising my internal profile. I know remote employees often suffer from the 'out of sight, out of mind' effect. Can you give me any insights on how 'visible' I am right now within our team and/or the business? Do you have any recommendations on what I could do to increase my visibility?" (This is also a great question to ask other people who work from home—they'll probably have strategies you can copy.)

168

CREATE A DAILY OR WEEKLY "WINS" LOG TO REFERENCE WITH YOUR MANAGER. Thanks to that "out of sight, out of mind" effect, it's important to proactively share your progress and accomplishments with your boss. At the end of each day or week (depending on the cadence of your projects), document your wins. Review this list before one-on-ones so they're top of mind—and then mention them! For instance, you might say, "We talked about X client last week, so I wanted to share an email they sent me. They're thrilled with the results we sent them. I think they're going to refer another branch of the company to us too."

169

ADD YOUR TEAM TO YOUR PROJECT MANAGEMENT TOOL. If you use Asana, Trello, Airtable, or another project management app to manage your workload and deadlines, give your boss and/or team members access to it. You can add them as users if they have an account, or send them the "view only" link if they don't. This hack saves you a ton of time: When someone needs an update on a task or project, they can quickly pull up the app and get the latest status instead of pinging you. (They'll also get a bird's-eye view of everything you're working on—which will squash any fears you're twiddling your thumbs at home.)

170

SCHEDULE A WEEKLY "NO MEETINGS" DAY. It's invaluable to have one workday each week to tackle meatier projects, get deep into your "flow state," and handle all the tasks you've been putting off. Choose a day that's typically lighter on meetings (Friday is a good bet) and block it off on your calendar. Depending on how normal this is for your company and team, you may want to get permission from your boss first. But be flexible about it. Occasionally, you'll need to have a meeting during your "no meetings" day. Name the calendar event something like "No Meetings Friday—please ask before booking!" so people know you're available if necessary.

171

**GIVE YOUR COWORKERS THE HEADS-UP ON POTEN-
TIAL INTERRUPTIONS.** If you know there's a decent chance
you'll need to take a call from your kid's school during a meeting, or run out in the afternoon to take a sick pet to the vet,
don't keep that information to yourself. At first, it might feel
weird to share personal details with your coworkers, but they'll
appreciate the transparency—and when the interruption does
happen, they won't be surprised.

172

HAVE "JOINT WORKING" SESSIONS. To re-create the
communal feeling of working together in one place, have
weekly one- to two-hour calls when the team switches on
their webcams while they work. This works best with silent
tasks, like coding, writing, editing, and so on. After everyone's
said hello and gotten settled in, encourage quiet by saying,
"Let's mute ourselves unless we have a question we want to
ask the group." To make the vibe more fun and casual, play
music. You can even take turns DJ-ing.

173

SET AN AWAY MESSAGE ANYTIME YOU GO OUT OF THE OFFICE. When you work in an office, your coworkers and boss always know about your out-of-office time—not only do you chat about your plans while you make coffee, stand at the printer, and take the elevator, but your empty desk or office reminds them you're gone. As a remote worker, you should overcommunicate your absence. Set an away email anytime you're leaving for two days or more. (If you don't want anyone who emails you to get this response, Gmail lets you set an away message only for people at your company and/or in your contacts.)

174

COORDINATE VACATION PLANS ON A SHARED TEAM CALENDAR. To make sure you've got appropriate coverage across the team, set up a calendar for vacations that everyone can edit. After their out-of-office time has been approved by their manager, they should add it as an event to the calendar. You can also use this calendar for communicating travel plans if people are temporarily working from different time zones.

175

LOOK AT A FILE'S ACTIVITY LOGS BEFORE ASKING IF YOUR COLLEAGUE HAS REVIEWED IT. This feature is available in most file management tools. (Just make sure you have edit access, or you probably won't be able to see the activity for a file.) To find it, click "Activity" in the sidebar (Dropbox) or top menu (Google Drive). If your coworker's name appears here, you have your answer.

176

GET AN OFFICE BUDDY. If some or all of your team works in the office, you might start to feel like the odd one out. Spontaneous conversations happen that you miss; people go out for lunch, coffee, or drinks together; and in meetings, you struggle to be heard over people who are actually in the room. An office buddy can help you stay up to date and visible. When a relevant discussion is happening without you, they can say, "Hey, should we make this a meeting so (your name) can attend?" When you can't get a word in during a call, they can create some space: "It looks like (your name) has a comment." Obviously, this needs to be someone you trust and has some clout, so pick the person you ask carefully.

HOW TO IMPROVE YOUR WRITTEN COMMUNICATION SKILLS

Like it or not, written communication became a major part of your job when you started working from home. Remote workers tend to use chat more frequently than in-office employees, and, because you don't have regular face-to-face time with other employees, the impact of your words matters more. If you write an unintentionally aggravating email, you can't patch things over with a brief chat. You might not even notice the email got a negative reaction in the first place, since you can't see the recipient's face or notice they seem a little less friendly in the hall than usual. All this is to say that strong communication skills will make you more successful at remote work. To up your writing game, try these ideas.

177

TAKE A BUSINESS WRITING COURSE. There are hundreds of virtual classes, covering everything from how to write proposals and reports to proofreading your work and using proper syntax and grammar. Figure out where you need to improve (your boss should be able to help) and look for a relevant course.

178

JOIN A WRITING GROUP. If you work in a creative field, this hack is a no-brainer...but it'll be helpful even if your writing is solely professional. Writing groups typically meet once or twice a month to share, discuss, and get feedback on their work. Some are in person; others are virtual. Most writing groups focus on creative work, not business writing; however, in the process of writing a novel, short story, or personal essay, you'll become an all-around better writer. A group will also make you better at giving and receiving critical feedback. If you have creative aspirations and want to meet others in the local writing community, this is a great option.

179

FIND A WRITING MENTOR. Ask your writing mentor to read and critique everything from drafts of important emails to memos to major presentations. They'll catch your mistakes ("This sentence is confusing") and identify recurring patterns ("You tend to bury your most important point in the second or third section"). It's helpful if your mentor works at your company so you don't need to worry about sending them sensitive information. If you're not sure whom to ask to mentor you, your boss might have some ideas.

180

SAVE EXAMPLES OF EFFECTIVE PROFESSIONAL WRITING FOR INSPIRATION. Create a folder on your computer or in the cloud; every time you come across a well-written piece at work, save it to this folder. Give it a descriptive label so you remember the type ("email," "proposal," "one-pager," etc.). Consider adding a few notes about its strong points so you can jog your memory later. Take a look at these examples:

» *Gets to the point*
» *Explains technical concepts simply but thoroughly*
» *Anticipates and dismantles potential counterarguments; very persuasive*
» *Doesn't get lost in the weeds—perfect for an executive audience*

Next time you're writing something important, find inspiration by reviewing similar pieces.

181

HIRE A WRITING COACH. This option isn't cheap, but it'll pay dividends over your career. A coach will work with you to identify focus areas, develop a personalized plan for addressing those areas, and give you ongoing feedback and advice. Ask your company whether they'll help finance a coach. If you're an executive, the organization may handle all the costs.

182

READ FOR FUN. It's no coincidence most great writers—professional or creative—are voracious readers. Reading improves your own writing skills by osmosis. You'll learn how to structure a sentence for maximum impact, which words convey the right emotion or meaning, how to persuade your reader without hitting them over the head with your point, and much, much more. For the best results, read a variety of authors, genres, styles, and topics.

183

USE A VIRTUAL WRITING ASSISTANT. Tools like Grammarly and ProWritingAid give you live recommendations on your style, grammar, tone, and more as you type—it's like having a writing coach looking over your shoulder. They integrate with popular Internet browsers, websites, office tools, and writing software, including Chrome, Safari, *LinkedIn*, *Medium*, Slack, Salesforce, JIRA, Microsoft Word, and more, so no matter where you're working, Grammarly and ProWritingAid are too. These are fantastic options if you're focused on the basics, but you may want to pursue others as well if you want more sophisticated recommendations.

• • •

184

DON'T SAVE YOUR FILES TO YOUR COMPUTER—KEEP THEM IN THE CLOUD. It's easy for information to get lost when everyone's saving files to their individual computers. If someone leaves the company or forgets what they named a file, you might never find it again. Plus, if multiple team members are working on a document, design, or presentation, their versions can quickly diverge. To save your team the hassle, use an online team file management tool like Dropbox, Google Drive, or OneDrive. These platforms make it easy to share, organize, and collaborate on every document your team needs.

185

WRITE A BRIEF PROGRESS REPORT BEFORE YOU LOG OFF. Shifts are pretty common for global developer and customer service teams. Don't ask the next shift to read through a huge backlog of messages that popped up while they were away. (Spoiler alert: They probably won't.) Before you call it quits, send a summary of what you or your entire shift accomplished, blockers you ran up against, questions you have, and any other pertinent info. This recap is also a nice way to collect your thoughts and tie up loose ends for the day.

186

GIVE SPECIFIC DEADLINES. You might feel awkward giving your peers due dates, but they'll appreciate the specificity. Knowing exactly when you need something done helps them prioritize the work and avoids confusion. To give you an idea, here's a too-vague request: "Can you take a look at this analysis before I send it to the rest of the team?" A better version: "Can you take a look at this analysis today before I send it to the rest of the team?" Best of all: "Can you take a look at this analysis sometime before 4 p.m.? I'm aiming to send it to the rest of the team by 5 today."

187

SKIP THE SARCASM. Sarcastic comments don't translate well over text. Maybe you want to playfully poke fun at your team's low energy, so you type, "Wow, glad everyone had their coffee today." No one can see your smile or hear your lighthearted tone, so they may assume you're annoyed. And even if you think your intention is obvious...you're probably wrong. A study published in the *Journal of Personality and Social Psychology* shows people commonly overestimate how effectively they communicate in writing. Next time you're tempted to use sarcasm, reconsider (and if you really can't resist, add an appropriate emoji).

188

GET EVERYONE ON THE SAME PAGE WITH A TEAM HANDBOOK. This handbook should list things like the following:

» The team mission and how you measure success
» Who's on the team and what they're responsible for doing
» The main communication methods your team uses and how quickly you expect responses for each
» The hours each person is typically online and any "core hours" when everyone's available
» Recurring meetings and/or stand-ups, and their purpose
» The tools you use and how to log in to them
» The chat channels or rooms specific to your team and their purposes
» Any other information that everyone should know

Not only will the handbook cut down on questions; it'll also help your coworkers standardize their processes and work more efficiently. You can send this handbook to new hires during the onboarding process as well.

189

GET THE LAY OF THE LAND BEFORE YOU START TALKING IN A NEW CHAT CHANNEL. You might be eager to participate, but you can get valuable context simply by scrolling up and reading the last fifteen or so posts. How formal or informal are people in this room? Do they use emojis and GIFs, or keep things professional? Do they rely on mentions to call out who their message is directed to, or let people figure it out for themselves? Do they share interesting links and articles, or do their conversations stay focused on work? Once you've gotten a feel for the room, you can tailor your style accordingly.

190

POSITION YOUR WINS AS LEARNINGS FOR THE ENTIRE TEAM. As a remote employee, intentionally highlighting your achievements helps you stay visible. But there's a fine line between promoting yourself and bragging. The key? Don't just say what you did—explain what you learned or why you think you were successful and how it can be useful in the future. Instead of saying, "Awesome news, everybody: The campaign I planned last month generated 150 percent of its lead goal," say, "The campaign I planned last month hit 150 percent of its lead goal! Just goes to show how finding the right co-marketing partner makes a huge difference. I'm wondering if we'll be able to utilize what we've learned here to…"

191

USE CHAT FOR DISCUSSION, NOT DOCUMENTATION.
Want feedback on a decision? Use chat. Need to document the decision you made? Record it via email or on your company wiki, knowledge base, or decision log. Chat shouldn't be your source of truth—it moves too quickly and gets too chaotic. With that in mind, move evergreen information to a platform people can reference for as long as necessary.

192

HAVE CONVERSATIONS IN THREADS. If you want to respond directly to someone's comment or point, don't send a message to the entire channel. Your coworkers will quickly get fed up with the flood of notifications. Threads also make it easier for people to quickly skim through the latest activity and see what they need to read and what they can skip.

193

ASK FOR A DEADLINE. If your coworker or boss doesn't provide a deadline along with their requests or assignments, don't be afraid to ask for one directly. Never assume you know how time-sensitive (or not) the task is. Say something like "I'm happy to do this. When should I get it back to you?"

194

DO A QUICK SEARCH BEFORE ASKING GENERAL QUESTIONS. Don't be the person who asks for information or a link that was already shared. Try a few variations on your search to make sure what you're looking for isn't easily found—then and only then, say, "Can anyone point me in the direction of X?" (If your company uses Slack, make sure to check out any pinned posts too. People usually pin commonly requested and important resources there. Unfortunately, this feature isn't available in other chat platforms yet.)

195

THINK TWICE (EVEN THREE TIMES) BEFORE USING @HERE. Your teammates will get irritated if you overload them with unnecessary notifications...so pause before you type @here, @channel, or @team (the last is specific to Microsoft Teams). Ask yourself, "Does everyone in this room—including people who might be sick, logged off, or out of the office—need to see this message?" The answer is no 99 percent of the time. (Don't forget, you can mention individual users if there are a few people who *do* need to see your message straightaway.)

196

FOLLOW THE MAXIM TO "PRAISE PUBLICLY, CRITICIZE PRIVATELY"...ESPECIALLY ON CHAT. Giving constructive feedback in a public channel should be avoided at all costs. After all, those comments won't just be visible to the other people in that channel—they'll also be searchable so the entire organization can find and read them. Plus, anything you write over chat is preserved forever. Comment publicly when you're recognizing someone's hard work or achievement, and save criticism for a direct message (or, better yet, a video call).

197

USE A PERSONAL CONTACT DATABASE TO MANAGE YOUR PROFESSIONAL RELATIONSHIPS. Most (if not all) of the interactions you have with your network happen virtually, making a central place to store information on your network valuable. You can create a record for every contact, logging basic facts like their location, job title, *LinkedIn* page, and contact details; your relationship to them; notes on your conversations, like commonalities or running jokes; and any other details that'll come in handy. Whenever you need to reach out to this person (or they reach out to you), pull up their name in your list, and you'll have all the information you need at your fingertips. Create a basic database in Google Sheets or try Monica or Airtable for a more powerful option.

198

ASK YOUR MANAGER AND PEERS FOR THEIR TOP FIVE CHANNELS. The older or larger a company is, the more channels it tends to have. Figuring out which ones you should belong to and keep up with is really tough—especially when you're remote and already somewhat cut off from the conversation. Track down any channels you should belong to by asking your boss and teammates which they read or participate in the most. If they exclusively name channels you already belong to, good news: You're fully in the loop.

199

FIND (OR CREATE) A CHANNEL FOR REMOTE EMPLOYEES. Most companies with multiple people who work from home have a chat room just for them: a place to share advice, commiserate about remote work challenges, pass on information, and more. This is a brilliant way to get to know colleagues across your organization, pick up valuable tips, and find a sense of community. If your company doesn't already have a channel set up—and you're not the only person working from home, of course—make one.

200

CREATE CHAT CHANNELS FOR COMMUNICATING WITH EXTERNAL FOLKS. If you have long-term relationships with agencies, freelancers, vendors, clients, or anyone outside your organization that you talk to often, create a channel in your platform of choice and invite them to it. They'll only have access to that channel—so don't worry about accidentally giving them visibility into your entire organization's chat. Now, all your communication will be in one place. (Not sure which relationships merit a channel? Keep an eye on your email inbox; anyone whom you've emailed five or more times in one week should get a channel.)

201

TAKE ADVANTAGE OF AUTO-TRANSLATION FEATURES. Perfect for global teams, Microsoft Teams offers in-line translation for thirty-plus languages, from Welsh and Lithuanian to Italian, German, Spanish, and French. In your settings, choose the language you want to translate messages into. When you want to translate an individual message, right-click it and select "Translate." While Slack doesn't currently offer its own translation feature, you can install Translate. This plug-in (which has free and paid plans) lets you turn on automatic translation for a channel or direct message—handy if you work frequently with a team in another country. You can also translate your own messages into another language by typing "/translate."

202

QUICKLY SURVEY YOUR TEAMMATES OR COMPANY WITH POLLS. Your response rate will increase dramatically when you start running polls over your chat instead of emailing people form links. Polly works with both Slack and Microsoft Teams and lets users set up everything from simple polls ("Where should we host our next team retreat?") to automated and individualized check-ins and surveys ("How has your first week at the company gone?" and "Do you have ten minutes to complete an employee feedback survey?").

203

CREATE LABELS FOR EACH OF YOUR TEAM MEMBERS AND/OR KEY CLIENTS. To make sure you can easily find all of your communication with every contact, and, more importantly, that you don't miss any time-sensitive messages, create labels that match each individual's email address. Check these folders for new messages before delving into the rest of your inbox.

204

PUT YOUR PRONOUNS IN YOUR EMAIL SIGNATURE AND CHAT PROFILE. For example, you might sign emails as "Aika, she/her," or "Kwan, they/them." Specifying your pronouns—no matter what they are—helps other people do the same and builds a more inclusive culture.

205

SET SLACK NOTIFICATIONS FOR YOUR KEYWORDS.
This hack will allow you to appear effortlessly whenever there's
a conversation happening that you should be involved in.
Consider creating notifications for the following:

» Any projects or programs you're leading
» Your name
» Your team name; for example, "Campus Recruiting"
» Processes or routines you don't want to miss, such as
  "expenses deadline," "company retreat," or "team
  all-hands"

To set up these notifications, click "Preferences," go to the
"Notifications" tab, and then enter your words and phrases
into the "Keywords" box.

206

**KEEP YOUR CHAT WINDOW UP ON YOUR SECOND
MONITOR.** This allows you to stay on top of notifications
as they come in while you focus on other work in your main
window. (Just make sure you're not getting too distracted by
the chatter.)

207

THINK BEFORE YOU CHAT. Here's an easy rule: If you wouldn't say something over email, don't say it over chat. Chatting with your colleagues feels pretty casual, so you're a lot more likely to voice thoughts or opinions that you wouldn't typically bring to work—especially if you're in nonwork-related chat channels. But remember, anything you write over chat is visible to your company's administrators, even if you're communicating via private channel or direct message. It's also preserved for eternity. Before you press "Send," picture the same message as an email. Is it appropriate? If not, hit "Delete" instead.

208

SPEND LESS TIME ON CHAT AND EMAIL WITH KEY-BOARD SHORTCUTS. It takes a little work to memorize which key combinations do what, but once you do, you'll save time every day. To see Slack's list of shortcuts, press "CMND" and "/" (Mac) or "CTRL" and "/" (Windows). To see Google Chat and Gmail's list of shortcuts, type a question mark (just make sure you're not typing in a text field). To see Microsoft Team's list of shortcuts, press "CTRL" and a period. Start by memorizing shortcuts to the actions you take the most: starting a new message, adding a status, running a search, and so on.

8 WAYS TO HAVE SOME FUN WITH YOUR OFFICE COMMUNICATIONS

Most of your communication in the office should be fairly professional and maybe even formal. No matter how you're communicating, whether it's via email, chat, or phone, always put your best foot forward. But you can still have fun with your coworkers! Try these hacks to add a little charm to your in-office messages.

209

"REACT" INSTEAD OF RESPONDING. It's faster to send and read an emoji than a written-out reply. If you use Outlook for email, you can "like" a message to indicate you've read it but don't have any specific action items to address. On chat platforms like Slack and Microsoft Teams, you can choose from a whole selection of emojis for your response. And if you've reacted to a message in a public channel, your team members can double-click your emoji to send the same reaction. Everyone participates more because it's so easy. Whenever your coworker shares positive news, makes a request, or posts something you want to acknowledge, start an emoji chain reaction.

210

USE EMOJIS. A few emojis go a long way: They soften a message, add personality, and help you build rapport with coworkers. However, if your colleagues rarely or never use emojis, you shouldn't either. And exercise good judgment—your boss probably won't appreciate a sad face when you say you're going to miss a deadline. If you do use emojis, save them for chat and skip them over email, since email is considered more formal.

211

THROW IN THE OCCASIONAL GIF. GIFs help you reinforce your team's culture and add some fun to your interactions. Use an appropriate GIF when your team is celebrating a win, having a silly conversation, or welcoming a new hire. That being said, you'll raise a few eyebrows if you use a GIF during a serious and/or more formal conversation. As a general rule of thumb, ask yourself, "Would I be embarrassed if the head of the company saw this message?" If the answer is yes, don't upload the GIF.

212

ENCOURAGE LIVELY CONVERSATIONS WITH YOUR CHAT STATUS. When you're not using your status to communicate that you're in a meeting, out of the office, or away, give your colleagues something lighthearted to discuss with you. Open-ended prompts like "Tell me your favorite karaoke song" or "Which actor would play you in a movie?" are fun icebreakers.

213

START YOUR OWN "STATUS TRADITION." Alternatively, write a daily status based on a theme. For instance, every day you could share a new interesting fact or riddle. Your colleagues will start looking you up just to read your status—and they'll always have something to talk about on your calls. However, this hack won't work for every company. If your organization is more buttoned-up, skip it.

214

ACKNOWLEDGE YOUR PEERS' CONTRIBUTIONS AND HELP IN A #SHOUTOUTS, #PEER-RECOGNITION, OR #GRATITUDE CHANNEL ON SLACK. This is a powerful way to build morale and encourage teamwork—and best of all, it's completely free. If a channel like this doesn't exist, ask your manager if you can create one. You'll brighten your coworkers' day by calling out their accomplishments.

215

CREATE A SHARED CALENDAR FOR CELEBRATIONS.
Add a little excitement to the calendar by including recurring events for each team member's birthday, work anniversary, and any other relevant dates (like the company's anniversary). Share this calendar with your coworkers so everyone knows who's celebrating a birthday or work anniversary and can send them a "congrats!" GIF or mention it in a meeting.

216

AMUSE YOUR TEAM MEMBERS WITH GOOGLE HANGOUTS EASTER EGGS. Next time you're chatting on Hangouts, type any of these commands into your window:

- » /shydino: triggers a shy dinosaur hiding behind a home
- » /puppyparty: sends a row of dogs to the other person
- » /roll: rolls a die
- » /bikeshed: changes the background color of your Hangouts chat window

Use them wisely, of course, but they can be a fun way to cheer up a coworker, share a laugh, or even make a simple decision (just choose "odd" or "even" on the die and roll away).

• • •

217

JOIN THE #POLITICS CHAT CHANNEL AT YOUR OWN RISK. At many companies, employees have started channels to talk about current events, upcoming elections, local politics, and more. And if you care about these topics, you're probably tempted to join! But here's the thing about political conversations: It's *too* easy to unintentionally offend or alienate people. Steer clear of these channels if you can or at least "lurk" behind the scenes without participating.

218

CRAFT IMPORTANT MESSAGES IN A GOOGLE DOC OR WORD FILE BEFORE SENDING THEM. This hack gives you a chance to perfect your message without any stress (just make sure you're drafting it somewhere you can't unintentionally press "Send"). Once you're happy with your message, copy and paste it into the appropriate channel, message, or email.

219

SEND MESSAGES TO YOURSELF FIRST TO SEE HOW THEY'LL COME ACROSS. Did you know you can send chat messages and emails to yourself? Just enter your name or email address (depending on the platform) into the "To" field and type your message like normal. You can proofread your message before you send it to its actual recipient. This is also a valuable hack for passing on bad news or relaying sensitive info: You can put yourself in the other's shoes and imagine how the message will read to them.

220

LET GOOGLE FINISH YOUR SENTENCES SO YOU CAN FLY THROUGH EMAILS. Thanks to Google's "Smart Reply" feature, which is available for Gmail and Google Hangouts, typing is easier than ever before. Turn it on in the "General" tab of your Gmail Settings: Scroll down to "Smart Compose" and choose "Writing suggestions on," and "Personalization on." When writing emails, Google will give you options to finish your sentence. You'll be surprised at how accurate the recommendations are—and the more you type, the better the suggestions become.

CHAPTER 4

OVERCOMING DISTRACTIONS

221

CLEAN UP YOUR WORKSPACE IN THE MORNING. If your home workspace doubles as living space, keeping it clean might seem impossible. Unfortunately, a mess makes it hard to get in the zone. Deal with this issue by establishing a short cleaning routine at the beginning of the day. When it's time to work, move anything from your nonwork life (like last night's wine glass, the bills you paid yesterday, or your guitar) into its proper place. Focus: returned.

222

BUILD UP "DISTRACTION DEFENSES." Make sure every member of your household who's old enough to take care of themselves understands when you're unavailable (like every day between 10 a.m. and 2 p.m., or anytime you close the office door). It sounds simple, but clear boundaries make a big difference. And once you've set those boundaries, stick to them as much as possible. Daily blocks of uninterrupted time will help you stay on task.

223

PUT A WHITEBOARD OUTSIDE YOUR OFFICE FOR NOTES. Ask your family, roommates, or partner to leave notes on a whiteboard during your off-limits time instead of texting you or knocking on the door. You're not interrupted; they know they'll get an answer. Win-win.

224

SET THE RIGHT EXPECTATIONS WITH FRIENDS AND FAMILY. People who have never worked from home sometimes treat it less seriously than in-office work—for instance, they might randomly drop by to say hi on a Tuesday afternoon or expect you to talk on the phone with them for an hour on a Wednesday morning. Let them know you're not available between 9 a.m. to 5 p.m. Monday through Friday (or whatever your working hours are) unless it's an emergency. This can be an awkward conversation, but it's a necessary one.

225

WALK YOUR LOVED ONES THROUGH A TYPICAL DAY. A rundown of all the meetings, tasks, and other work you do on a daily basis helps people understand working from home really does mean *working*. Let's say someone is frequently testing your boundaries (like repeatedly calling you in the middle of the day after you've asked them to please respect your work hours, or getting upset that you can't spend time with them during the workweek). Say, "Can I give you a quick overview of my typical daily (workload, routine, work-from-home schedule)? We've talked about my job but not the day-to-day, and I'd love for you to have that context." That'll give them a better idea of what you're doing and why you're unavailable even if you're at home.

226

PRACTICE SAYING, "I HAVE X MINUTES TO TALK" AND "I NEED TO GET BACK TO WORK." Stopping for the occasional quick chat is okay—after all, it's normal to exchange small talk with your coworkers when you see them in the kitchen or hallway—but don't fall into the trap of hour-long conversations when you need to work. At first, it might be difficult to cut off your roommate or neighbor—especially when it *looks* like you've got all the time in the day to talk—but the sooner you get in the habit of politely but firmly ending the conversation, the better.

227

SET TIME LIMITS ON INTERRUPTIONS. Always getting sucked into chats with your partner or roommate, Internet black holes, games on your phone, or other distractions? Give yourself a firm time limit (ideally five to ten minutes). To make sure you get back to work when time is up, set a timer on your phone or keep an hourglass on your desk. A timer or hourglass is also handy for ending conversations; just say, "That's my cue! Let's pick this up when I'm done with work at X time."

228

GET A "DO NOT DISTURB" SIGN. A closed door is the universal signal for "I'm busy, please don't bother me." But if you don't have the benefit of a separate room for working, create the same effect with a "do not disturb" sign on your desk. And be consistent about enforcing your "do not disturb" times—you have to train the other members of your household that the sign actually means you're unavailable.

229

CREATE A SMART LIGHT SYSTEM THAT'S TIED TO YOUR CALENDAR. Technology can do incredible things—like telling the people you live with that they shouldn't interrupt you. Buy a colored smart light (ideally red, since everyone knows what that means), place it outside your office door or near your workspace, and connect it to your calendar app using an event-based automation tool like IFTTT or Zapier. Trigger the light to turn on when you're booked for meetings and/or deep work. When the light is off, you're open to interruptions; when the light is on, you're not. This takes a bit of work to set up, but once you have, the people you live with will never barge in again. It's the ultimate "do not disturb" sign.

230

USE REMOTE-CONTROLLED LIGHTING TO SIGNAL WHEN YOU'RE BUSY. For an alternative lighting solution you can set up in half an hour, buy a remote lighting kit. Plug in the light next to your desk or outside your door. (For the latter, make sure your remote is powerful enough to work through walls.) Whenever you don't want interruptions, use the remote to turn the light on. When you're happy to chat, use the remote to turn it off again.

231

HAVE A HOUSEHOLD MEETING EVERY MORNING. This "meeting" doesn't have to be formal—five minutes while you sip your morning cup of coffee or tea is perfect. Compare your schedules, priorities for the day, and any shared responsibilities so you can figure out any compromises or handoffs you'll need to make. For instance, if you have a big meeting from 10 a.m. to noon, you might ask your roommate if you can use the office during that time frame since it's quieter than the den. Maybe the plumber is coming by in the afternoon; you're happy to let them in since your partner (who also works remotely) was planning to head to a coffee shop after lunch. Perhaps someone needs to get poster board for your kid's project; you can do it if your spouse can pick them up from camp. This quick meeting ensures nothing will fall through the cracks.

232

SHARE YOUR CALENDAR. Whether you're cohabitating with a roommate, relative, partner, or some combination thereof, sharing your calendars makes it easier to juggle meetings and other obligations. This is especially important when one person is using a common space to work or you're both in the same room. To share a Google calendar, hover over its name in the "My calendars" section and click "More" and then "Settings and sharing." Scroll to "Share with specific people" and select "Add people." (The person you're sharing with needs to have a Google account as well.) To share an Outlook calendar, click "Share" and choose the appropriate calendar. Then enter the email address of the person you want to share it with. (They need to have an Outlook.com or Microsoft 365 account to accept.)

233

CREATE A CALENDAR FOR ANY SHARED WORKSPACES. Then book them when you need the room. Name the calendar after the room or space: "Kitchen table" or "Basement office." When you need the space, add "Kitchen table" or "Basement office" to your meeting invitation. If it's already taken, you know your roommate or partner is using it. In addition, you're less likely to interrupt each other because you'll know what areas of the house to avoid or when to be as quiet as possible.

234

COORDINATE SCHEDULES ON A WHITEBOARD. Go analog and use a whiteboard to track your schedules. That way, if your roommate takes a quick look at the whiteboard and sees you're in a meeting until 12:30 p.m., they'll know to hold off on asking you about lunch plans until then. Plot out the entire week or just that day, depending on how far in advance you know which meetings and other obligations you'll have. This is a visual way to see when two or more people have calls at the same time—and it also lets you easily assign household chores and other responsibilities. It's an especially useful exercise for parents and two-plus remote employees in the same household.

235

ROTATE WORKSPACES. There's probably one spot in your home that's best for meetings or deep work—the Wi-Fi is reliable, it's quiet, and there's a nice setup for video calls. When you live with someone else who works from home, switch up your workspaces so you get equal time in the prime area. If you have multiple workspaces in your home, try assigning slots based on the day of the week or time period (mornings, afternoons, or evenings). You can schedule your deep work or meetings for times you know you'll have a disruption-free block.

236

TRACK YOUR TIME TO FIGURE OUT WHEN AND HOW YOU'RE GETTING DISTRACTED. Using a time-tracking tool like Toggl, Clockify, or Harvest gives you insight into your personal productivity. You'll learn how many minutes you spend on work versus distractions, which websites pull you out of work mode, and which times of day your mind typically wanders. Use this information to course-correct. Once you've tracked your time for a week or two, use the patterns you've seen to create a personal productivity strategy.

237

GIVE YOURSELF NEW PERSPECTIVE—LITERALLY—BY CHANGING LOCATION. When you don't have time for an extended break, reset your focus with a new work spot. Finding yourself staring into space at your desk? Take a quick walk to a nearby coffee shop, museum café, coworking space, or restaurant (just make sure they have Wi-Fi, if you'll need Internet). If you can't go that far, take your laptop into your backyard or head to the kitchen table. You can even try sitting in a different chair than your usual one. It might sound minor, but looking at something new will often give you a burst of motivation.

238

CHANGE YOUR PLAYLIST. This is a great hack for combating distractions, since simply switching up your tunes can help you refocus. For an even more powerful mental reset, change genres—and pay attention to which songs or artists help you concentrate so you can come back to them.

239

SHARE YOUR CHORE MANAGEMENT STRATEGY WITH THE OTHER MEMBERS OF YOUR HOUSEHOLD. If you decide you won't do chores during the workday, make sure your roommate(s), partner, children, and so on know the deal. That way, you won't get interrupted with requests to take out the trash, go grocery shopping, or tidy up, and can instead focus deeply on your work.

240

TURN OFF THE TV. Tempted to stream a show or movie while you work? You're not alone: *Netflix* found nearly four in ten people have watched TV while working. But unless you're using it purely for background noise, this habit isn't helpful. Multitasking is a myth; you'll always produce better work when your attention is focused on one task alone.

241

PUT YOUR PHONE OUT OF SIGHT. You won't be tempted to scroll social media if your phone is tucked away in a drawer or different room. This also compels you to take a quick break (and get some steps in) every time you want to check it.

242

USE YOUR WORK LAPTOP FOR WORK AND ONLY WORK. Not only does your company probably prefer it, but your bookmarks, most-visited sites, and top apps will all be work-related too—which helps you avoid temptation when you get the urge to check social media or surf the web. You'll also create a stricter division between your work and personal life, which lessens the feeling of always being "on."

243

USE A SEPARATE INTERNET BROWSER. If you don't have two laptops, achieve a similar effect by designating one browser for work and one for play. On your work browser, bookmark your company email, intranet, knowledge base, industry resources, and so on. On your personal browser, bookmark the nonwork equivalents, like your personal email and favorite websites. As soon as you're done working for the day, switch browsers.

244

MAKE YOUR PHONE LESS ADDICTING BY TURNING OFF THE COLOR. Tristan Harris, founder of the Center for Humane Technology and former Google designer, says this hack can reduce the constant desire to look at your phone. After all, color grabs your attention—gray does not. iPhone users can find the grayscale option in settings, under "Accessibility" and then "Display & Text Size." Toggle "Color Filters" on, and choose "Grayscale." Android users can do the same by adding the pen icon to Quick Settings and simply tapping the pen to go gray.

245

BUILD THEMED TO-DO LISTS. It's easy. Just pick a productivity hack that works for you and build your to-do list around that "theme." For example, maybe moving to different locations helps you stay on-task. Create a to-do list based on places to work. Pick locations that are within walking or driving distance of each other so that each time you finish the items for that location, you can easily move to the next one. Or maybe different playlists help you get in the right mindset. You might have one playlist for simple, straightforward tasks, another for projects requiring deep focus, a third for creative work, and more. When you move from one task type to the next, change playlists accordingly.

246

ANSWER EMAILS MORE INTENTIONALLY WITH EMAIL BATCHING. Rather than keeping your inbox open all day, devote two or three blocks of time to reading and responding to messages. Between these blocks, keep your inbox shut. Your productivity will go up when you're not reading and responding to new messages every ten minutes.

247

BAN THE "SAD DESK SALAD"—OR "SAD DESK ANYTHING"! Even if you work in an office, eating meals away from your desk is a good idea: It lets you decompress, enjoy your food, and move around a bit. When you're working from home, these benefits become even more important. You'll have an easier time focusing throughout the day if you give yourself a half or full hour for lunch.

248

OUTSOURCE AS MUCH AS POSSIBLE. Overwhelmed by keeping the house clean? Hire a cleaning company. Too busy to cook? Sign up for food delivery. Can't keep up with laundry? Pay for pickup and drop-off service. While outsourcing your household tasks is pricey, it's a solid investment if it makes you more efficient, focused, and calm.

249

USE YOUR HEADPHONES TO SIGNAL WHETHER YOU'RE OPEN TO INTERRUPTIONS. Create a system with the other members of your household: If you're wearing your headphones, you're unavailable; if you're not wearing them, you're open to questions, quick conversations, and so on.

250

GET A WHITE NOISE MACHINE. If you don't like wearing headphones while you work, a white noise machine will provide a soothing soundtrack of ambient sounds. As a bonus, you can also turn on the white noise machine at night to help you sleep. (For a budget-friendly alternative, use a fan.)

251

USE A DISTRACTION-FREE TOOL FOR WRITING. Having trouble concentrating on the memo, email, blog post, or project recap you need to write? There's an app for that. Tools like OmmWriter and Calmly Writer are designed to boost your focus by stripping out all but the most essential features of a text editor. If you prefer to write in Microsoft Word, try Focus mode. Go to the "View" tab, then click "Focus." (Depending on your version of Word, you might need to click "Immersive Reader" in the "View" tab instead.) Focus mode is a full-screen, immersive experience that blocks out everything on your screen but the page.

252

SAVE INTERESTING ARTICLES AND WEBSITES FOR LATER. It's hard to stay in the zone when your coworker sends you a blog post to check out or you come across an intriguing link on *Twitter*. Use an app like Pocket or Google Keep to save these links to a virtual library. When you're ready to take a break, they'll be easy to find.

253

MUTE BUSY OR LESS-RELEVANT CHAT CHANNELS. You could probably spend half your workday—if not more—keeping up with new messages on your workplace chat. To make sure you're seeing only the most important notifications, use the "mute" feature for extra-noisy channels on platforms like Slack. Instead of getting an alert for every new message, you can do a "drive-by" whenever you want to catch up.

254

REGULARLY AUDIT THE CHAT CHANNELS YOU'RE IN. If you haven't participated in (or learned important information from) a channel in the past four-plus weeks, leave it. You can always rejoin it if you need to, but in the meantime, you'll have fewer notifications to distract you. Slack makes this hack even easier by sending you notifications when you haven't used a channel in a while.

255

MEDITATE FOR TEN TO FIFTEEN MINUTES A DAY TO IMPROVE YOUR ABILITY TO IGNORE DISTRACTIONS. Meditation has tons of mental health benefits, including better focus and productivity. And you don't need to spend hours a week meditating to reap the rewards—according to a study published in 2017, just one fifteen-minute session can reduce mind-wandering by 22 percent. Best of all, unlike office workers, who rarely have a quiet, private place to meditate during the workday, you can meditate in your bedroom at any time.

256

USE A WRITING APP TO ENTER FLOW STATE. The Most Dangerous Writing App is a free online tool that lets you set a session length from three minutes to sixty. Once your session begins, you have to write and *keep* writing—because if you don't type anything for five seconds, all of your work will be lost. You can even turn on Hardcore mode to blur out everything you've already written so you're not tempted to go back and edit. Flowstate is a less-stressful alternative; this iOS app simply doesn't let you press "delete."

257

GIVE YOUR ATTENTION TO IMPORTANT NOTIFICA-TIONS. Do you have hundreds of unread notifications? Only spend time on the ones that matter. Here's an easy way to prioritize them: First, go through all of your private messages and respond to whatever you need to (or set a reminder to respond to them later). Then check out the most recent messages from any high-priority channels, like the one with your direct team. After you've done that, mark the remaining unread messages as read. You've just given yourself a clean slate.

258

SEND EMAIL NEWSLETTERS TO A SEPARATE FOLDER OF YOUR INBOX. If you subscribe to multiple industry, current events, or media newsletters, you might be overwhelmed by how quickly they pile up. To avoid inbox overload, put them in a separate folder. You can either create a rule to send emails from specific aliases (for example, noreply@getpocket.com) to an "Email Newsletter" folder. Or send any email that contains the word "Unsubscribe" to the folder (although this filter will catch *all* mass emails, including marketing ones).

259

SCHEDULE DEEP WORK SESSIONS. If your job involves deep work (which could be anything from writing code to drafting a memo to designing wireframes to analyzing data), block out focused time. Add a one- to three-hour event to your calendar so you don't get booked in any meetings. When the session begins, turn off your notifications; hide your phone (if it's not already in a separate room); tell your roommates, partner, and/or kids you're unavailable; and get into the groove. Remember to update your chat status and calendar so your team knows you haven't gone MIA.

260

USE DIFFERENT DESKTOPS FOR DIFFERENT TASKS. Giving each project its own window forces you to tackle one thing at a time. If you can't see the number of unread messages in your email ticking up, you won't get distracted or anxious. Best of all, you don't need multiple screens for this hack—many computers come with the ability to tab between two-plus desktops. Create and manage desktops on a Mac by pressing "Control" and the up arrow and clicking the plus icon. Do the same for Windows by choosing "Task View," then "+ New desktop."

261

ASK A FRIEND TO KEEP YOU ACCOUNTABLE. You can partner up with a coworker, former colleague, or even friend. Every morning tell each other your productivity goals (for example, "I want to accomplish X and Y" or "I want to spend less than thirty minutes on social media") and then check in with each other at the end of the day. Knowing you'll have to report your progress to another person makes you likelier to follow through.

262

BLOCK OUT DISTRACTING SOUNDS WITH NOISE-CANCELING HEADPHONES. These will help you maintain focus while your neighbors do construction, kids play in the street, your partner practices the tuba in the next room, or your roommate blasts their music.

263

SET MESSAGE REMINDERS FOR YOURSELF. Tools like Slack give you the option of reminding yourself about a message in twenty minutes, three hours, the next day, or a custom period of time. Use this to put a pin in conversations so you can concentrate on your current task without stressing you'll forget to respond.

264

USE EXERCISE TO RESET. Going for a quick walk or jog is a reliable way to boost your energy and take a time-out from thinking—so when you get back to your desk, you can double down on your to-do list. If you've only got a few minutes, do some jumping jacks or push-ups.

265

SPLIT MAJOR DEADLINES INTO SMALLER, MORE MANAGEABLE ONES. It's easy to lose your focus when you're tackling a project with a distant due date. *What's the harm in checking social media?* you think. *I've got weeks to finish this.* Next thing you know, the deadline is three days away and you're scrambling. Avoid the last-minute rush by breaking down your high-level projects into concrete steps and assigning a deadline for each, such as "Create outline by X date" and "Flesh out outline by Y date."

TIPS FOR WORKING FROM HOME AS A PARENT

Many people go remote *because* they have children. Remote work gives you more flexibility and a lot more time at home, making it easier to spend time with your kids and, well, take care of them. But let's be honest, working while your kids are home is tough. Your parental responsibilities can often interfere with your work ones—especially if you've got a young one (or more than one) running around. Use these hacks to minimize distractions while still being a present and loving parent.

266

TEACH YOUR KIDS HOW TO PACK THEIR OWN LUNCHES. This hack can save parents a ton of time in the morning. And, if you need to send out a few emails before dropping your kids off at school, you'll get a few interruption-free minutes while they're busy. To encourage your children to make healthy choices, give them a formula to follow (e.g., one vegetable, one fruit, one protein, and one sweet treat).

267

REWARD POSITIVE BEHAVIOR. If there's a specific behavior you want your children to develop, consider giving out rewards when they successfully complete that task. Maybe they remembered to play far away from your office when your door is closed for a meeting or fixed their tablet issue independently while you were on an important call. A small prize will teach them to repeat that behavior going forward. Use a sticker chart for little kids and a points- or token-based system for older ones.

268

ROTATE CHILDCARE RESPONSIBILITIES WITH YOUR PARTNER. This technique allows one remote worker to focus on professional tasks while the other remote worker takes care of the kids. It's not always easy to pull off, but if you can, your productivity will thank you. Perhaps you have a big client meeting at 2 p.m., while your partner has a free time slot. Ask them to keep an eye on the kids until 3:30 p.m. so you can be at your best during the meeting. The next day, when your partner needs to catch up on a project, you can take the kids to the park. Try to balance the ratio of professional to caretaking time between you and your partner over the course of the month so neither of you neglects your job.

269

SET YOUR ALARM (EXTRA) EARLY. Consider waking up before your kids to give yourself some buffer time. Not only will this give you time for focused work; you might also enjoy the peace and quiet.

270

PICK ONE TO THREE WORK PRIORITIES. Every morning, write down a list of what *must* get done that day, and tackle that list before anything else. If the kids need a lot of attention in the afternoon or you're bombarded with lots of little distractions, you'll still have accomplished the essentials. This strategy will also keep your workload in check—if you're tackling the most important tasks, you'll never get so far behind that you can't catch up.

271

TEACH YOUR KID(S) HOW TO PREPARE THEIR OWN SNACKS AND DRINKS. Instead of asking you for snacks throughout the day, let your kids handle snack time on their own. If they're young, put out a snack "buffet" with healthy prepackaged food they can grab at any time. Otherwise, show your kids how to prepare a safe, healthy snack on their own.

272

TRY OUT TIME BLOCKING. If you're a parent or caretaker, you might need an ultra-flexible schedule. Fortunately, working from home lets you divide your day into blocks of time dedicated to specific tasks. This technique helps you stay focused, work more efficiently, and manage both familial and professional obligations. Schedule blocks for both types of responsibilities throughout your day; for instance, you might have a morning block for kid-related tasks, followed by a meetings block, another for answering emails, an afternoon block for your children, and a final block for writing memos, creating presentations, and so on. If you try time blocking, make sure to give your team members and manager the heads-up about your availability.

273

CUT YOURSELF SOME SLACK AROUND SCREEN TIME. Need your children to stop screaming while you're on a work call? Pull out the iPad. But skip the guilt: You're doing the (near) impossible by simultaneously parenting *and* working. Choose an educational show or game (or on rough days, whatever your kid will happily stay glued to) and give yourself an uninterrupted hour of work.

274

BRING IN REMOTE ENTERTAINMENT AND EDUCATION.
Looking for a fantastic way to keep your kids busy when you
need some time to focus? Have someone else provide the
entertainment. Thanks to web-conferencing tools like Zoom
and Skype, you can hire any entertainer or instructor with an
Internet connection. Pay a magician to perform, an artist to
teach watercolor painting, or another professional who can
lead your kids through an age-appropriate activity they can do
independently. And, if you're working in the same room, you
can keep an eye on your child.

275

GET A REMOTE "BABYSITTER." This hack works best if
your kids are a little older and have the attention span to stay
engaged with someone on-screen. Ask the grandparents or
family friends to "hang out" with your young ones while you
knock out a key task or take a call.

· · ·

276

PUT DECISIONS ON AUTOPILOT. Every choice you need to make—whether it's big, like "which technology should we use for this project?" or small, like "what should I have for lunch?"—fatigues your brain and drains your concentration. Save your mental energy for the important questions by eliminating as many recurring decisions as possible. Follow the same schedule every day, meal prep so your breakfast and lunch are ready to go, and use an automation tool like Zapier or IFTTT so routine tasks happen in the background.

277

DESIGNATE A PET-FRIENDLY AREA. Working from home with a dog? Now you'll have extra time to spend with your pet—woohoo! Unfortunately, dogs don't understand "do not disturb" signs. With that in mind, invest in some toys and a separate place for your pet to hang out during the day. A toy will keep them engaged while you're in meetings (although if they wander into the frame, it's not the *worst* thing in the world), and keeping them in an area away from your work-space helps you focus and teaches them clear boundaries.

APPS TO HELP YOU BATTLE DISTRACTIONS AND STAY IN THE ZONE

Technology is often responsible for pulling you off track, but it can also help you maintain concentration. First, figure out what your biggest productivity obstacles are. Do you have a hard time reading "just one" article or resisting the urge to check the score? Are you sidetracked by loud noises? Do you succumb to the siren call of social media?

Once you know what you're up against, pick out the tools on this list that'll help you get in the zone—and stay there.

278

BLOCK OUT EXTERNAL SOUNDS AND BOOST YOUR FOCUS. Brain.fm (iOS and Android) and https://focusmusic .fm (online) are like Pandora for work music. Unlike most songs, which try to get your attention, these songs are crafted to exist in the background.

279

REPEATEDLY REMIND YOURSELF TO STAY FOCUSED. The Momentum (Chrome) extension asks you to enter your daily goal; once you do, you'll see that goal every time you open a new tab.

280

GET INTO THE ZONE WITH BACKGROUND NOISE. Apps like Noisli (iOS, Android, Chrome, and online) and Noises Online (online) let you mix and match calming sounds (like rain, birdsong, campfire, etc.) to create your perfect blend of background noise.

281

LOCK YOURSELF OUT OF DISTRACTIONS ON YOUR PHONE AND COMPUTER. Unlike other options, Freedom (iOS and Windows) can block both websites and software programs. It also syncs across your devices so you can't cheat by using your phone or tablet.

282

ENCOURAGE YOURSELF TO STAY ON TASK BY VIRTU-AL "GARDENING." Try using Forest (iOS, Android, and Chrome). You plant a virtual seed that grows into a tree over the course of thirty minutes...unless you go to one of the sites on your "blacklist," in which case, your sapling dies.

283

THINK TWICE BEFORE YOU GET DIVERTED. Pause (Chrome) is a free extension that makes you wait five seconds before going to a website you've earmarked as a distraction.

284

LIMIT YOUR BREAKS. Try StayFocusd (Chrome), Leech-Block (Chrome, Firefox, and Microsoft Edge), or Waste-NoTime (Chrome and Safari) to help you cut back on your favorite time-wasting sites. You can set custom time limits for each site you'd like to spend less of your day on.

285

CURB YOUR SOCIAL MEDIA USE. Feedless (iOS) actually removes your feed of content from *Facebook*, *Twitter*, and *Instagram*. You can still friend or follow other users and post your own content—you just can't see what anyone else has posted. For a similar effect, Chrome users can install News Feed Eradicator, which does the same thing for *Facebook*.

286

GET RID OF TABS YOU DON'T NEED. Having too many open tabs can be a distraction—and increases the likelihood that you'll check out *Facebook* if it's already open in the background. The OneTab (Chrome and Firefox) extension turns all of your open tabs into a hyperlinked list of pages so you can easily come back to the ones you need to. No chance of "accidentally" opening *Instagram*...plus your screen will look cleaner and your computer will run faster.

287

CRAFT A DISTRACTIONS-FREE WORK ENVIRONMENT.
Serene (MacOS) prompts you to define your goal and sub-
goals for the day. When you start a work session, the app
blocks distracting websites, updates your Slack status, turns
your phone to silent, and even changes your lighting and finds
a focus-boosting playlist. Perfect conditions for a deep work
session.

288

TURN YOUR TO-DO LIST INTO A GAME. The Habitica app
(iOS and Android) gives you rewards for sticking to your goals
and crossing off tasks. You can even compete with your friends.

. . .

289

USE AS FEW TOOLS AS POSSIBLE. There are thousands of
helpful apps out there. The key is to choose what works for
you; don't try to use them all! It's harder to stay focused when
you're constantly switching from tool to tool—not to mention, you'll spend a lot of time and energy trying to figure out
where you saved something and moving information from one
place to the next. Every app should play at *least* one key role.
For example, maybe you track events, to-dos, and reminders
in Google Calendar, send emails in Gmail, and take notes and
save inspiration and ideas in Evernote.

CHAPTER 5

MEETING REMOTELY

290

PUT YOURSELF IN THE BEST LIGHT—LITERALLY. To look your best on video calls, find a source of natural light: It'll illuminate your face without the harsh effects of artificial light. Aim to sit directly in front of your natural light source. If that's not possible, sitting diagonal to it works as well.

291

KEEP LIGHTING CONSISTENT. For best results, stick to one type of light. Ideally, your natural light source is bright enough. If it's not, point a desk or task lamp at the wall in front of or next to you to get a diffused light that'll mimic natural light. (This hack only applies to meetings; during the rest of your workday, use a combination of lights as needed so you can easily see what you're doing.)

292

COPY THE EXPERTS AND GET A RING LIGHT. *YouTube* stars and pro videographers rely on ring lights for great lighting every time. Like the name suggests, a ring light is a circle-shaped light that casts an even, flattering, shadow-free glow on your face. They cost between $20 and $200. Note that you'll need to mount your camera at the center of the ring light. You can use your phone if you don't want to spend any more money, or buy a webcam if you're looking for a professional-level setup.

HOW TO EFFECTIVELY AVOID DISTRACTIONS IN A MEETING

When you're actually in the room, you're typically more focused, more aware of how others are behaving, and more conscious of how your actions might reflect on you. Unfortunately, remote workers have to work harder to avoid distractions and gauge how others are feeling. Connecting via video call also means you have less control of what's going on around you, like your dog's barking, roommate's music, or neighbor's lawn mower. Although you can't completely get rid of these distractions, minimize them with these tips.

293

REMOVE AMBIENT NOISE WITH NOISE-CANCELING SOFTWARE. Once you install software on your computer that removes background noises, you'll never again have to apologize to your coworkers for sirens, screaming children, banging pots and pans—or any other sounds that might disrupt your meeting. Try Krisp, which works with more than eight hundred apps (including Zoom, Google Meet, and Skype).

294

TAKE NOTES THE OLD-FASHIONED WAY. Spare your coworkers from the sounds of typing by jotting down notes on a physical notepad versus a digital one. As an added benefit, this will help you avoid the temptation of your email or the web.

295

SILENCE YOUR PHONE. Always make sure you turn off the sound before your meeting begins. Better yet, put your phone into airplane mode—or shut it off completely, if you struggle to stay focused. Seeing or hearing notifications pop up will take you out of the zone...and your coworkers will usually notice.

296

DISABLE TEXT, CHAT, AND EMAIL ALERTS ON YOUR COMPUTER. Notifications on your laptop are just as disruptive as phone ones. Maybe even worse, because it's easier to check them: All you have to do is click. Plus, you never know when you'll need to share your screen—why run the risk of having your coworkers see a silly text from your friend or gripe from another team member? You can easily avoid these issues by turning off all notifications before you hop onto a call.

297

DON'T HAVE REMOTE MEETINGS IN COFFEE SHOPS. Or any public place, for that matter. You shouldn't discuss any sensitive information where strangers are in earshot. Even if the meeting topic is completely straightforward, the other meeting attendees might still feel self-conscious. Taking calls in public is also rude to the people sitting around you. And if those weren't reasons enough, the coffee shop's background noise is distracting.

298

GIVE THE MEETING YOUR FULL ATTENTION BY GOING FULL SCREEN. During calls, remote workers need to be even more present than in-office employees. However, they're also battling more distractions. To stay focused on the meeting—and *just* the meeting—make your web conference window full screen. Your participation, ability to stay focused, and memory of what you talked about will go up, since you can't see your other windows. This hack will help you look engaged from the beginning of the meeting to the end, since your coworkers can tell when you're checking your email if your eyes slide away or the light from your monitor flickers.

299

HIDE YOUR OWN VIDEO ON ZOOM CALLS. Looking at your own face on video is distracting—instead of engaging fully in the discussion, you're fixing your hair, thinking about your posture, or analyzing your facial expression. To get rid of your thumbnail on *your* screen only (meaning the other meeting attendees will still see you), right-click it. A menu should pop up; choose "Hide Myself." If you want to get your thumbnail back, right-click again and choose "Show Myself."

· · ·

300

PUT YOURSELF IN THE CONFERENCE ROOM WITH A 360-DEGREE VIDEO CAMERA. It's tough to be the sole remote participant in a meeting. It feels like you're interrupting instead of participating naturally, you have less presence than the folks physically in the room (literally), and you struggle to hear what everyone is saying. Enter the Meeting Owl from Owl Labs. This all-in-one camera, mic, and speaker sits in the middle of the conference room table and acts as your eyes, ears, and voice. The camera automatically focuses on the person speaking, so it's easy for you to follow the conversation; plus, with multiple mics and an extended pickup range, you'll never miss another word. The Meeting Owl is an investment, but it's worth it if you're the only remote employee on your team.

301

CHECK (AND RECHECK!) YOUR SCHEDULE. To avoid last-minute cancellations or schedule changes, review your upcoming meetings, phone calls, and check-ins at the beginning of every week, looking for potential conflicts. (Depending on how often your schedule changes, you may need to do this throughout the week as well.) It's more polite to reschedule or cancel two to four days out.

302

REGULARLY AUDIT YOUR MEETINGS TO IDENTIFY THOSE YOU CAN STOP HAVING. Recurring meetings have their own momentum. Even if you don't *need* to meet, you do because...well, it's on the calendar! And once you're in the meeting, people usually find ways to fill the space. To win back valuable time from unnecessary meetings, review your recurring ones once a quarter. Ask yourself, "Would I schedule this meeting if it didn't exist?" If the answer is no, ask the host if they're open to moving the discussion to chat or email by saying, "Hi (their name), To free up everyone's schedules, what are your thoughts on replacing this meeting with a Slack or email update?" If you're the host, send a message to all attendees: "Hi all, To give everyone (amount of time) back, let's move this to (chat, email). Please let me know if you have any concerns. If I don't hear from anyone, I'll take this off our calendars."

303

REACH OUT BEFORE YOU SEND THE MEETING INVITATION. If you want to meet with someone outside your usual orbit—like, say, someone several levels above you in the corporate hierarchy or a peer you want advice from—ask in advance so they're not surprised by a random calendar invite. Your message can be quick; think, "Hi so-and-so, I'm (your name) on the such-and-such team. I'd love to get your thoughts on X. Are you open to meeting for thirty minutes to chat?"

304

KEEP A FEW MEETING ALTERNATIVES UP YOUR SLEEVE.
The more creative you get with communication methods, the
fewer meetings you'll need to schedule. Here are a few ways
to pass on information or updates without hopping on a call:

» Start a thread on chat or within your project management
tool to get short updates from everyone on your team.

» Send out a survey if you're looking for feedback on a
completed project, team or company initiative,
or general employee engagement.

» Turn on "Suggesting" or "Track Changes" in a Google Doc
or Microsoft Word file, respectively, if you're providing
feedback on someone's memo, project overview,
experiment summary, and so on.

305

**AUTOMATICALLY UPDATE YOUR SLACK STATUS TO RE-
FLECT WHEN YOU'RE BUSY.** Once you've connected your
Slack account with your Google Calendar or Outlook account, your status will change to "in a meeting" with a calendar icon during every block you're booked. Colleagues can see
at a glance whether you're available to jump on a call. They'll
also understand you might take longer than usual to answer
any messages. And you won't have to manually update your
status ten times a day as you jump in and out of meetings.

306

AVOID "ZOOM FATIGUE" BY SHARING A "MEETING CHECKLIST" WITH YOUR TEAM. Zoom fatigue is a real thing: According to researchers Libby Sander and Oliver Bauman, virtual meetings require more mental processing power. You need to pay close attention to nonverbal signs like facial expressions, body language, and gestures that you'd normally pick up on and interpret subconsciously. You can't look away, since you'll look distracted or bored. Any audio lag can make conversations sound stilted. And you feel like you're on display, since you never know who's looking at you. To prevent "Zoom burnout," share the following checklist with your team, either verbally or as a PDF that they can print and post near their desk. They should only schedule a meeting if they meet *all* of the following qualifications:

» The group needs to make a decision.
» You can clearly articulate what that decision is.
» That decision requires input from the entire group.
» That input must be given in real time.

307

DON'T CANCEL (OR EVEN RESCHEDULE!) MEETINGS THE DAY OF. While virtual meetings might *feel* more casual than face-to-face ones, they're just as important. People carefully plan their schedules around meetings, so you'll mess up their plans if you cancel or reschedule at the last minute. As a general rule of thumb, don't cancel or move meetings scheduled within the next ten hours. If canceling is unavoidable, send a note to the other attendee(s) explaining why (you're sick, you were just booked in another meeting at the same time, you have a personal obligation, etc.). If the meeting time is simply inconvenient, take one for the team and don't change it, even if you have to reorganize your schedule to make it work.

308

TAKE ADVANTAGE OF THE EVENT INVITATION OR DESCRIPTION SO PARTICIPANTS KNOW WHAT TO EXPECT. The more advance information your attendees have, the better: They'll know what to expect, and you'll look organized and prepared. Along with the agenda, required prep work (if any), meeting length, and date and time, include whether you're talking over phone or video. If it's the former, include the phone number and meeting code, and if it's the latter, let them know which software they'll need. It's also a good idea to specify whether cameras will be on or off.

HOW TO PREVENT REMOTE MEETING TECH ISSUES

Nothing derails a meeting more quickly than your video lagging, freezing, or disconnecting entirely. Fixing these issues eats up valuable time and throws you off-course. Use these tips to make your meetings run smoothly and help you keep your composure.

309

DO A SPEED TEST. There are tons of free tools online that'll let you test your Internet connection (just Google "speed test"). Running a test fifteen or so minutes before your meeting starts gives you the chance to troubleshoot the issue.

310

RUN A TEST MEETING. Some web conferencing tools, like Zoom and Webex, let you do a dry run using their test site. Head to https://zoom.us/test or www.webex.com/test-meeting.html to check your video and audio connection. If you're on Skype, test your audio by calling the "Echo/Sound Test Service" contact in your contacts list. Using a tool that's not on this list? Start a call with yourself.

311

MAKE SURE NO ONE'S WATCHING *NETFLIX*. If anyone else on your Wi-Fi network is eating up lots of bandwidth—streaming and gaming platforms are common culprits—ask if they'll take a break until your call ends. This will free up your connection for the meeting.

312

TRY A NEW ROOM. Believe it or not, metal objects, plumbing, and other electronics might be interfering with your Wi-Fi. Switch up the room you're in and see if that helps the connection.

313

TURN OFF YOUR VIDEO. Video freezes during your presentation to the C-suite or sales call with a potential customer? Don't panic. Say that you're going to turn off your video. (You may need to repeat this message in the meeting chat if your audio is having issues.) That'll free up some of your computer's bandwidth, which should improve the latency problems.

314

CALL IN. If you're still struggling with a weak signal after trying any (or all) of these other fixes, you might need to call in. Many web conference platforms will let you join a video meeting by phone. Let the other meeting participants know your plan, exit the meeting, grab your phone, find the meeting phone number and PIN (if it's not in the invite, ask the organizer to send it to you), and dial in. You'll be back in the discussion in less than three minutes.

315

USE YOUR PHONE AS A MOBILE HOTSPOT. If your Wi-Fi is flagging and you don't want to dial in, go to your phone's settings and make sure your personal hotspot is enabled. Then go to the Wi-Fi settings on your computer and look for your phone's name. You may want to charge your phone while it's tethered to your laptop—using it as a hotspot will quickly eat up its battery.

316

REBOOT YOUR ROUTER. Sometimes, the most effective way to resolve Internet issues is also the easiest: Simply turn off your router (or unplug it if it doesn't have a power button), count to ten, and turn it back on again.

· · ·

317

ADD TIME ESTIMATES FOR EACH ITEM ON YOUR AGENDA. This best practice is even more important for remote meetings, where it's easy for the conversation to go off the rails or the loudest participants to dominate. If you'd like specific people to talk and/or prep for different sections, note that too. Here's an example of a well-written agenda:

» Overview of project goals: Siena (5 min)
» Summary of technical challenges: Ellen (10 min)
» Break out into three groups of three to discuss: Everyone (20 min)
» Presentation of each group's favorite idea: Everyone (15 min)
» Next steps: Adam (5 min)

318

SAVE MEETING RECORDINGS TO A TEAM OR COMPANY FOLDER. To make information easy to find across your team, department, or company, put meeting recordings in a folder everyone has access to. Let's say your employee misses your weekly all-hands—instead of bugging you for the recording, they can simply go find it in the folder.

319

HIDE THE MESSAGE IN YOUR NOTIFICATIONS. If you're going to keep the notifications coming while you're on calls (which isn't recommended but might be necessary for your job), update your settings so only the sender shows up—not the message itself. Imagine you're sharing your screen and a Slack notification pops up from your coworker: "Did you read Kellan's latest email? What's a professional way to say, 'All of these ideas are horrible'?" or you get a text from your partner: "How did the conversation with HR about your boss go?" At best you'll be embarrassed, and at worst you'll harm your work relationships. But these hypotheticals will *stay* hypothetical if you change your notification settings for all the communication platforms you use ASAP.

320

MAKE MEETING AGENDAS A COMPANY-WIDE POLICY. Basically, if there's no agenda, there shouldn't be a meeting. Since an agenda is so critical to a well-run meeting, avoid showing up to or hosting conversations that don't have one. Even a one- or two-sentence description of the meeting's purpose is better than nothing. Institute a company-wide policy that all meetings must have an established agenda visible to every participant. If you can't come up with an agenda, that's a sign that you don't need a meeting and can probably get the necessary info through other communication channels.

321

ROTATE MEETING LEADERS. Anyone can play this role—in fact, you may want to rotate who moderates each time if it's a recurring meeting. The leader is in charge of guiding the discussion, calling on participants, and sending out the recording or follow-up notes after. Having a leader does a few things: It keeps the meeting on track, ensures you hit all the discussion points you need to without going over time, and ensures you'll remember to record and/or take notes. Rotating your meeting leaders means that everyone will have the opportunity to participate and practice important leadership skills.

322

DESIGNATE A TIMEKEEPER. Do your meetings often run over schedule? Ask someone to be the timekeeper. This person is responsible for communicating how many minutes each participant has to speak and letting them know when they're close to—and at—time. The timekeeper is essential for discussion-based meetings, large meetings (think eight-plus attendees), and meetings with strict agendas. It also improves the odds that everyone will get time to speak, particularly if some attendees are notoriously chatty or long-winded.

323

RECORD MEETINGS BY DEFAULT. Even if you're taking notes, it's helpful to record your meetings. You never know when you'll need to refresh your memory on a specific decision, catch another colleague up to speed, or rewatch an explanation of a tricky concept. The one exception to this rule: Any meeting where you'll be discussing confidential or sensitive information should not be recorded. People are far likelier to speak honestly during unrecorded sessions. (That doesn't mean you can't take notes or refer back to statements they made during these meetings, of course.)

324

SPEED UP RECORDINGS TO SAVE TIME. Tools like Zoom and Loom let you watch videos others have shared with you at faster speeds. Start with 1.5x, which is fast enough to save you a significant amount of time per meeting without making people sound like chipmunks. However, if you don't mind the squeaky pitch, and you can absorb everything you hear, go up to 1.7x or even 2x. If you're not able to attend a meeting and need to catch up on the recording later, this hack will help you zoom through the audio (pun intended).

325

ENABLE AUDIO TRANSCRIPTION FOR INSTANT ZOOM MEETING NOTES. After you turn this feature on, you'll get an automatic audio transcription of any meeting or webinar you record—with time stamps! Go to your portal and select "Account Management" and then "Account Settings." Find the "Recording" tab and scroll to "Advanced cloud recording settings." Check the box marked "Audio transcript." (Note that you must be an administrator or account owner and have a Business, Education, or Enterprise license to use this feature.)

326

REWATCH MEETING RECORDINGS AND PAY ATTENTION TO HOW OFTEN YOU PARTICIPATE. As a remote employee, make sure you're visible and actively participating in (virtual) conversations. But striking the right balance is important: Are you overcompensating for being remote by speaking up *too* much and not leaving enough space for others? To get an idea of where you stand, rewatch meeting recordings and try to be objective. Maybe you're dominating the conversation. Or maybe you're on the other end of the spectrum and aren't speaking enough. Ideally, everyone should be getting roughly equal airtime. Once you know where you fall, recalibrate if necessary.

327

MONITOR YOUR SPEAKING STYLE. Rewatching meeting recordings lets you gauge how effectively you're making your points. Look at the other attendees' reactions when you talk. Are they nodding, or do they look confused? If it's the latter, why? Is your language clear and concise? Do you use industry jargon or make references your audience might not understand? This exercise is a little uncomfortable, but your speaking skills will improve every time you do it.

328

KEEP THE LIST OF ATTENDEES AS SHORT AS POSSIBLE. The more people on a call, the harder it is to manage the conversation. So, invite as few people as possible. In general, that's two to four people for an open discussion, five to eight people for a guided one, and nine-plus people for presentations, announcements, and any other meeting where a few people are talking while the rest of the group is listening. If your invite list is longer than ideal, ask yourself if every person truly needs to attend—or if there are some people you can update afterward.

329

MAKE MEETINGS AS SHORT AS POSSIBLE. The conversation tends to expand to fill the allotted time. If you have fifteen minutes to discuss something, you'll take fifteen; if you have thirty minutes to discuss the same topic, you'll probably take thirty. Always book the shortest amount of time you can. Worst-case scenario: You need to book a follow-up meeting. Not sure what "as short as possible" means? Use these rules of thumb:

» **Daily stand-up:** twenty minutes
» **Weekly one-to-one:** thirty minutes
» **Weekly status meeting:** thirty minutes for eight people or fewer; forty-five minutes for nine to twelve
» **Brainstorming session:** forty-five minutes
» **Biweekly one-to-one:** forty-five minutes
» **Presentation:** thirty minutes to an hour, depending on the topic's scope and discussion plans

330

MAKE TIME FOR INTRODUCTIONS. Introductions help you ease into the meeting and are especially important for voice-only conference calls. At the beginning of the call, the meeting leader can kick off introductions by asking everyone to share their name and title. If the leader forgets, say, "Looks like we've got some new folks on the line—should we do intros?" or "I don't think this group has met before. Can we do a quick round of names?"

331

ROTATE THE ORDER OF SPEAKERS FOR RECURRING TEAM MEETINGS. Changing up who speaks first, second, third, and so on ensures the same people don't always get stuck with the undesirable last speaking slots—which tend to be shorter than everyone else's.

332

PUT CHATTY TALKERS NEAR THE END OF THE AGENDA. If you notice someone is consistently talking too much—but you're not in a position to ask them to be more concise—put their section at the end of the meeting so the rest of the speakers have a chance to talk first. For discussion-based meetings, call on them after others have spoken.

333

CAP ALL MEETINGS AT ONE HOUR. It's nearly impossible for people to stay focused and engaged for longer than sixty minutes. Plus, there are few topics that require this much time to discuss. Look at the meeting agenda and see if there are any sections that can be delivered in a different format, like a prerecorded video or a memo. If you're doing an all-day discussion, retreat, or internal conference, cap individual sessions at sixty minutes and give people ten to twenty minutes in between to decompress and reset.

334

KEEP YOURSELF UNMUTED DURING MEETINGS WITH FOUR ATTENDEES OR FEWER. It can make you look antisocial or disengaged to turn your sound off when it's just you and a few other people. However, if you're worried about ambient noise, ask the others, "Hey, can you hear (X sound) in the background? Is it distracting?" If they say yes, it's fine to mute yourself for as long as the sound continues.

335

TAKE ADVANTAGE OF THE MEETING CHAT. You can quickly send your coworkers a high five, deliver information, crack a relevant joke, or ask the speaker a question without interrupting the verbal discussion. And if you're more comfortable typing than talking, it's also an effective way to participate.

336

PLAY DISCUSSION TAG. This simple exercise helps everyone get a chance to speak. Once someone is finished speaking, have them call out or "tag" the next speaker. Ask people to raise their hands or use another visual cue to indicate they have something to say. The current speaker should prioritize people who haven't talked yet. Discussion tag makes the conversation feel balanced and keeps things interesting.

337

DIVIDE LARGER GROUPS INTO BREAKOUT PODS. Brainstorming and discussion sessions can spiral out of control when you've got more than five participants. To keep unstructured conversations productive, split everyone out into groups of two to five. If your meeting platform doesn't support breakout sessions, create individual meetings for each group. After everyone's gotten the rundown in the larger meeting, send them to their smaller pods to discuss further. If you need to regroup to wrap up the discussion, ask everyone to rejoin the larger group meeting.

338

MUTE YOURSELF IF YOU'RE CONTRIBUTING LESS THAN 20 PERCENT OF THE TIME. Use this hack for presentations or larger meetings with a lot of people present. Unless you want to distract and frustrate your colleagues with random sounds, keep yourself muted on calls where you're participating less than 20 percent of the time. The only exception is when someone is giving a presentation and you want to encourage them with auditory feedback, like laughter, snaps, claps, "hmms," and so on. Just make sure you're in a quiet place to avoid unwanted background noise.

339

MUTE LARGE MEETINGS BY DEFAULT. If you're hosting a large meeting, turn this setting on—it'll prevent a flood of random noises as folks join. If you're using Zoom, click "Participants." At the bottom of the window that pops up, choose "Mute All." Zoom will ask if you want to let participants unmute themselves; select "Continue." If you're using GoTo-Meeting, click "People" to open the list of attendees. At the bottom of the window, select "Mute All."

340

SHOW TWO TIME ZONES IN YOUR CALENDAR. This feature is helpful when you regularly meet with people in another office or location. It shows what time your meeting will be in your area versus your colleague's area, so you can schedule a time that works well for you both. To turn it on in Google Calendar, go to "Settings," click "Time zone," check the box labeled "Display secondary time zone," and then pick the appropriate one. You can even add a label, like "Erica—Dublin" or "Japan team." To enable multiple time zones in Outlook, click "File," "Options," and select the "Calendar" tab. Then scroll down to the "Time zones" section and check the box labeled "Show a second time zone."

341

USE VISUAL CUES TO SIGNAL WHEN YOU WANT TO TALK. Seeing who's about to speak is challenging when you're not in the same room—plus, video typically has a small lag. Fortunately, you've got lots of alternatives if audio clues aren't working. Try raising a virtual hand emoji when you want to say something, turning "mute" off (the other participants will see your screen icon change from "muted" to "unmuted"), or typing a quick note in the chat to get the leader's attention.

342

USE A FUNNY PROP TO INDICATE YOU WANT TO SPEAK. Perfect for an informal meeting, this hack helps you have a little fun while you come up with new ideas. If your team is having a brainstorming session, ask everyone to find a funny hat, costume glasses, or another type of wearable prop. When someone wants to talk, they put on their hat, glasses, and so on; when they're done, they take the prop off. Not only will it be easy to run the discussion, but everyone will get a chuckle too. You might even feel a bit more creative and energized...essential elements of a successful brainstorm.

343

TAKE YOUR WHITEBOARD TO THE CLOUD. In many ways, virtual whiteboards (like the ones you can create with Miro or Microsoft Whiteboard) are better than physical ones. You can add files and links directly to your digital board, have multiple people drawing on it at the same time, and, when you're done, quickly and easily save and share it. Give everyone a link to the board and a prompt and ask them to add their ideas before your discussion; alternatively, for a "live" brainstorming session, schedule a call where you can all talk and update the board at once.

344

USE AN APP TO FIGURE OUT THE IDEAL MEETING TIME.
If participants are scattered across multiple time zones, look
for a slot that'll be convenient for as many people as possible.
Ideally, it should fall during every participant's normal work
hours. If that's not possible, prioritize a time that's convenient
for the maximum number of people *or* that avoids anyone
having to wake up super early or stay online into the wee
hours. To avoid doing a bunch of napkin math, use an app (like
the free Meeting Planner tool from www.timeanddate.com or
Miranda for iOS) to plug in everyone's locations and get a list
of suggested times.

345

**ROTATE MEETING SLOTS FROM MORNING TO EVE-
NING.** Sometimes you can't find a slot that's within normal
working hours for every participant. When that's the case, try
to take turns getting the "desirable" slot—for example, if you
meet at 9 a.m. your time and 6:30 p.m. your colleagues' time,
the next meeting might be at 7:30 a.m. your time and 5 p.m.
your colleagues' time.

346

BE EXPRESSIVE. Because it's harder for your coworkers to read your body language or facial expressions, hold your gestures a little longer and make them a little more obvious. And, if you're on mute in a large group, your verbal response will go unheard. So if someone is presenting, nod to show you like their points. If they share good news, do a little dance, pump your arms, or clap.

347

DON'T FORGET ABOUT HOLIDAYS IN OTHER COUNTRIES. If you're working with an international team, your public holiday schedules will be different. Keep this in mind when you schedule meetings or map out project timelines. To add another country's public holiday dates to your Google Calendar, go to "Settings" and select "Holidays." Then add the appropriate country. To add multiple country holiday schedules to Outlook, click "File," "Options," select the Calendar tab, find "Add Holidays," and check off every country you need.

348

ASK FOR QUESTIONS EARLY AND OFTEN. When you're not sitting in the same room with your coworkers, they're shyer about speaking up when they have a question or comment. Counteract this by periodically saying, "Does anyone have any thoughts before I move on?"

349

GIVE YOURSELF A SUBTLE GLOW-UP ON ZOOM. Zoom offers a discreet filter that'll make your face look brighter and smoother. It's a good hack to use when you're short on time but need to look put together. To turn on this filter, go to "Settings." If you're on your desktop app, choose "Video"; if you're on your phone, go to "Meetings." Then check the box labeled "Touch up my appearance." This feature will stay on by default, so if you only want it for one meeting, remember to go back and uncheck it after.

350

RESERVE TIME FOR SMALL TALK. Spend at least five minutes at the beginning of every call shooting the breeze. It might feel unproductive, but without the watercooler conversations that happen spontaneously in the office, these five minutes are some of the most important of the meeting. Informal conversations help you build rapport, get to know your colleagues on a personal level, and create a sense of camaraderie. And when you need to have a difficult or sensitive discussion, it'll be far more effective if you've built strong relationships.

351

ALWAYS CLOSE WITH A FOUR-SENTENCE RECAP.

This gives you a chance to clear up any miscommunications—which are more common during virtual meetings than in-person ones—and gets everyone motivated. Four sentences are perfect for summarizing what happened and what's coming next. Try this formula: "We talked about A, B, and C. Our ultimate goal is Z. We decided (name/team) would do X by (date), and (name/team) will do Y by (date). We're going to (meet again/ check in on) Z day."

352

MAKE YOUR COWORKERS LAUGH (OR YOUR DARK CIRCLES DISAPPEAR) WITH SNAPCHAT FILTERS. Once

you've downloaded Snap Camera (Snapchat's desktop app for Mac and PC), you can select it as your webcam device in Zoom, Skype, Google Meet, Google Hangouts, and more. Amuse your team members with funny filters, or subtly touch up your appearance with beauty ones.

353

PRETEND YOU'LL HAVE TO GIVE YOUR BOSS A CLIFFSNOTES SUMMARY OF THE MEETING. This strate-

gy will help you stay engaged and, maybe more importantly, focused on the conversation's highlights. Feel free to actually take notes.

354

PREP QUICK "SOUNDBITES" FOR SMALL TALK QUESTIONS. It's a guarantee: Every Monday morning meeting will start off with the question "How was your weekend?" Come prepared with a few one-liners to share with your colleagues; for instance, "I went hiking with my dog," "I started a fantastic new show," or "I made pasta from scratch." With these ideas up your sleeve, you won't end up saying, "My weekend was good; how was yours?" Instead, you can spark an interesting conversation and get to know your coworkers and their interests. On Wednesday, think of two or three responses to "Any fun plans this weekend?" to keep the conversation going.

355

SAY OTHER PEOPLE'S NAMES TWICE PER RESPONSE. Acknowledging them by name shows respect; plus, it makes *you* look more engaged. Just don't go overboard—if you're dropping someone's name every other sentence, you'll seem disingenuous. As a good rule of thumb, use someone's name two times in each response: once when you start talking, and once when you end. For example, "It's Valentina. I'd like to explore what Patrick just mentioned. I've noticed... Curious to hear everyone's thoughts, and thanks for bringing that up, Patrick."

356

LEARN HOW MUCH YOU'RE SPEAKING WITH MEETING TRANSCRIPTS. You might suspect that you need to speak up more often—or, on the flip side, that you hog the limelight. You can review a recording of the meeting...unless your company doesn't record or share all meetings, or you don't want to listen to the entire meeting again. With software like Gong .io or Otter.ai, you can easily gauge your participation rate. Add one of these apps to your call (making sure you've gotten everyone's permission to record). After the meeting is over, you'll get an automated transcription of it. Learn instantly how many times you participated and for how long. As a bonus, you'll have detailed, searchable notes of the meeting too.

357

START WITH YOUR CAMERA OFF. If you're not sure whether the people you're meeting will have their cameras on or off, start the meeting with yours off. Once the other participants have joined, follow their cue: If they're using video, quickly switch your video on too. If they're not using video, keep yours off. This lets you avoid the awkwardness of being the only person on camera. You can even make this your default setting in your web-conferencing settings if you use Zoom. Go to the "Video" section of preferences and check "Turn off my video when joining a meeting."

358

NAIL IMPORTANT PRESENTATIONS BY PRERECORDING.
Giving a talk to an extra-large or important audience, like the
entire company, the executive team, or even a few hundred
external folks? Filming it in advance ensures things don't go
awry: Your kids won't burst into the room halfway through,
your audio won't lag, your video won't freeze, your graphics
will work...you get the gist. Streaming a prerecorded video also
lets you answer questions live in the meeting chat. Not only
will the presentation still feel interactive; this is also a better
way to do a Q and A than waiting until the end or interrupting
your talk track to answer questions.

359

**MAKE PRERECORDED PRESENTATIONS INCLUSIVE
BY ADDING CAPTIONS.** Filming your speech or demo in
advance also lets you add closed-captioning and/or subtitles—
which makes it accessible for attendees with hearing impair-
ments or for non-fluent speakers. Video caption services like
Rev, GoTranscript, and Scribie are fairly affordable, accurate,
and quick. Of course, if you're on a budget, you can also add
captions yourself.

360

WRITE DOWN YOUR QUESTIONS AND COMMENTS.
And then wait for the appropriate time to jump in with your contribution. Once you've recorded your thought, you'll feel less pressure to voice it instantly; you know you won't forget what you were thinking. People can tell when you're waiting for them to finish so you can talk, so be respectful and listen carefully to what they're saying.

361

VOLUNTEER TO WRITE UP YOUR TAKEAWAYS FOR THE REST OF YOUR TEAM. Going to a department or company-wide meeting? You'll build goodwill with your team and give yourself a reason to pay close attention to the meeting (which can be difficult to do if you're a passive participant). Try doing this for recurring meetings that not everyone can attend.

362

MENTION YOUR NAME EVERY TIME YOU SPEAK UP IN A CONFERENCE CALL. For example, you might say, "This is Hazeem. Adding onto your point, Sadie..." or "Hazeem here. I'd like to give some additional context to what Sadie just said." Saying your name ensures everyone knows who's speaking—which is harder to keep track of than you'd think when there are several voices on a call.

363

CREATE ONE MEETING "ROOM" FOR BACK-TO-BACK CALLS. If you're meeting with a bunch of different people back-to-back, make it easy on yourself by creating one meeting for the entire time. Use Zoom's or Skype's "waiting room" features (found in "Group Management" and then "Meetings," and "Meeting Options," respectively) to let in each person you're meeting with at the appropriate time. If they try to join the meeting before you're ready for them, they'll get a message asking them to wait until the host admits them. You can seamlessly move from one call to the next without worrying about finding the right link, entering the password, and so on. This hack is particularly useful for running interviews, sales calls, or customer service consultations.

364

PROTECT YOURSELF FROM "ZOOM BOMBING" BY LOCKING THE MEETING ONCE IT BEGINS. All Zoom meetings are now password-protected by default, which has stopped hackers from crashing meetings and causing chaos. If you want to be extra careful, go to security settings once the meeting has begun and select "Lock Meeting." No one else will be able to join, even if one of the attendees shares the meeting link and password.

365

USE THE PRES FRAMEWORK TO GET TO THE POINT. It's even harder to hold people's attention over a virtual meeting. If you have trouble speaking clearly and concisely, try organizing your thoughts into the following categories. Keep it to a sentence or two for each point so you can move along quickly...and look highly organized.

» **P:** the Point, or your main idea
» **R:** the Reason, or why your idea makes sense
» **E:** the Example/Explanation, or how your idea manifests itself
» **S:** the Summary, or what to do with the idea

366

USE YOUR ZOOM "NAME TAG" TO KICK-START CONVERSATIONS AND BUILD RAPPORT. To update your meeting title, click "Participants," find your name, select "Rename," and then edit away. If you're meeting with a bunch of people for the first time, you might want to list your team, title, and/or location. Or add a fun, work-appropriate detail about yourself. This is also a great feature to use in more informal situations: If you're playing a team game, make your Zoom title your competitive persona, such as "Ava Attack" or "Carlin 'the Champ' Martin."

367

CALL ATTENTION TO THE TIME TO KEEP MEETINGS MOVING ON SCHEDULE. Listening to someone drone on and on while you watch everyone's eyes glaze over and the clock tick down is excruciating. Don't let it get that far—you'll be doing everyone a favor. Next time a colleague is rambling, politely say, "Thanks (name). In the interest of time, should we (table this topic for now, have so-and-so give their thoughts, move to the next discussion item)?"

368

PAUSE AFTER MAKING A POINT. Your powerful point will get lost if you don't. However, when you're nervous (or chatty by nature), it can be tough to stop speaking. Take a deep breath and force yourself to go silent so others can react.

369

AVOID SMALL TALK BY USING UNIQUE CONVERSATION-STARTERS. Instead of asking people, "How's the weather in your neck of the woods?" or "Planning any trips?" pose interesting, lighthearted questions like "What's the last TV show you stayed up late to finish?" or "Settle a debate for me: Is a hot dog a sandwich?" Going beyond boring surface-level topics will deepen your connection—which will make the rest of the meeting more productive.

CHAPTER 6

MANAGING REMOTELY

370

PRIORITIZE WEEKLY ONE-ON-ONES. Since your reports can't physically see you in the office or lean over to ask you questions, your total communication time generally drops. Catching up with them individually once a week will keep motivation and productivity high and make you feel present. Schedule a thirty- to forty-five-minute meeting, depending on how much support each report needs. And once they're on the schedule, make those one-on-ones your number one priority—don't skip or reschedule them. When your schedule starts looking tight, it's tempting to make things work by canceling or moving one-on-ones, but this sends a powerful (and negative) message to your team: Your meetings with them don't matter. With this in mind, reschedule one-on-ones only when you have no choice, and never cancel them completely.

371

COCREATE THE AGENDA. Use this hack when you're co-presenting or meeting with only one other person (like during your one-on-ones). You can use a shared Google document, the calendar invitation for the meeting, or meeting management software—whatever will be easy for both of you to access and update. This hack ensures you're both prepared for the meeting in advance and gives you a written record of what you discussed.

372

PROTECT YOUR TEAM'S CALENDAR. Every month or so, skim through each report's calendar and see how much time they spend in calls each week. Do they have enough un-scheduled time to get non-meeting work done? For individual contributors, at least 65 percent of their day (if not more) should be open for independent work. For managers, that should be 30–65 percent, and for leadership, 30 percent. If your reports aren't getting enough time, work with them to cancel unnecessary recurring meetings and say no to more invitations.

373

HOST OFFICE HOURS. Open your virtual door for an hour every one to two weeks so your reports have a chance to ask questions, get guidance or clarification, solicit feedback, or simply get to know you. Try to keep this time on the books no matter what—you can always work on other tasks if no one shows up. Have a few activities or thought exercises in mind in case people come but don't have much to say. For example, if one of your reports needs help brainstorming ideas for a new social media account, you might pull from a list of customizable, open-ended questions like "If I gave you a blank check and asked you to show 50 percent growth by X date, what would you do? Now, how can we make that idea doable for our business given Y constraints?"

374

TAKE A BREAK. If you take vacation time, your team will be empowered to take their own. Make sure you're getting off the grid as frequently as you advise them to do so (anywhere from two to eight weeks per year). And broadcast that you're away! Since people can't register your absence by looking at your empty desk, it's extra important to update all of your channels. Give your reports the heads-up in your team-wide meeting, remind them in your individual check-ins, set up an away message for your email, and change your chat status to "OOO" (out of the office).

375

SCHEDULE YOUR EMAILS INSTEAD OF SENDING THEM AT OFF HOURS. If you send emails or messages over the weekend or late at night, your reports will read them. To avoid giving the impression you expect them to work around the clock, try to send messages between 8 a.m. and 6 p.m. Monday through Friday. Ideally, this time frame will also force *you* to take a time-out after hours and on the weekends. However, if you do end up drafting an email or message over the weekend and are worried you'll forget about it if you don't press "Send," many email platforms will let you schedule a message for the future. Or, you can simply save the draft and set a reminder to send it for 9 a.m. on Monday.

376

MAKE YOUR CALENDAR PUBLIC. This encourages transparency and gives your team visibility into how you spend your time (many people have no idea what their manager does on a daily basis, especially when said manager is not physically around). Of course, keep in mind your industry, company culture, and role—if most or all other managers keep their schedules private or your work is highly sensitive, leave your schedule locked.

377

KEEP A RUNNING LIST OF ALL THE TOOLS YOUR TEAM IS USING. Every three to six months, look at your list and consider the primary purpose of each program or app. Forcing yourself to define every app's purpose will keep you organized and help you spot overlap. To give you an idea, perhaps you realize you're using two separate tools to manage your projects. Figure out which works best for your purposes and phase out the other. You can also ask everyone on your team to fill out a quick form or update a spreadsheet with the software they're using regularly. That way you'll be able to gauge if people are using different tools for the same purpose, if *more* team members should be using specific tools, and if team subscriptions or licenses would save you money. This exercise streamlines your team's tool kit (improving communication and collaboration) and frees up some budget.

378

ADD PERSONAL EVENTS TO YOUR CALENDAR. Within reason, of course. Scheduling life obligations and errands empowers your direct reports to craft their own work-life balance. When they see you're taking, say, an hour on Thursday to interview a music teacher for your child, or forty-five minutes every morning to work out, they'll feel more comfortable taking their own breaks.

379

ADVOCATE FOR MENTAL HEALTH DAYS. Make it clear to your team that they don't need to go anywhere to use vacation time; they can take a day or two off at any point to relax and recharge. When someone is visibly stressed or worn out, nudge them to take a mental health day or plan some vacation time. The best strategy, of course, is leading by example. Taking a mental health day yourself normalizes the practice—especially if you share how it impacted your energy levels and engagement when you come back.

380

DON'T WAIT TO DEAL WITH PERFORMANCE ISSUES. No one likes having a difficult conversation about performance issues, and the virtual distance can make it easier to put it off. If your report seems less engaged, motivated, or productive than normal, don't wait and see if the situation improves. The longer you delay, the larger the issue will become. In addition, the rest of the team will wonder why you're letting poor performance slide—which can hurt morale. A couple of key points to remember:

» Have difficult conversations over a video call, not chat or email. If you can't see their face and body language and hear their tone, you're bound to misinterpret something they say (or vice versa).

» Create a safe space to discuss issues virtually. It's often harder to be vulnerable with a face on a screen versus another person in the room, so tell them you want to resolve these issues *together*. Immediately letting your team member know you're on their side will put them at ease.

» Don't record sensitive or performance-oriented meetings. You want to create a psychologically safe space so your report feels comfortable opening up. Recording the call will have the opposite effect.

» Dig into the "why" of performance issues. Remote work is challenging—especially if you're a newbie. Consider the possibility this person is struggling because they're working from home. To dig into the issues, ask probing questions like "What's your biggest obstacle to (achieving X, producing work at Y quality, hitting your deadlines for Z)?"

381

CREATE A SET OF CORE VALUES FOR YOUR TEAM. Culture is harder to create and maintain on a team when the leader (and potentially others) are remote. That means you need to deliberately shape it. As a team exercise, write a code of values. Do this *with* your team so that the values feel authentic and people buy into and support the ideas. Try asking everyone to submit one to three statements—such as "Put users first, then the team, then yourself" and "Never sacrifice your life for work"—and then vote on their favorites. This manifesto will help formalize your culture and encourage employees to follow the principles.

382

CREATE TEAM AWARDS. To drive your team or company's values home, give an award every month to a team member who's demonstrated one of those values. If your team is big enough, consider having peers nominate one another. Make sure to explain why this person got the award so everyone can see your values being lived out; for example, you could say, "Sam's receiving the award this month for 'acting like an entrepreneur' and 'providing true value.' He came up with a creative solution to a big problem when he...."

383

MONITOR WORK OUTPUT, NOT HOURS. Since you can't peek over your reports' shoulders, employee monitoring software may seem like an alternative solution. Yet tracking your team's every keystroke is horrible for morale: It makes people feel (and rightfully so) they're being surveilled. As long as they're performing at the level you'd expect, who cares if they're spending a half hour on *YouTube* every once in a while? Plus, it's not a good use of *your* time to pore over a breakdown of who visited which sites or typed less frequently than someone else. Evaluate each person's performance on the quality and quantity of their work—not how they spend their time.

384

DOCUMENT EVERY ISSUE WITH AN EMAIL. Even if you don't record a meeting about your employee's performance, you still need a paper trail. If there's any disagreement down the line, you can refer back to your messages—and if you end up putting this person on a performance plan or terminating them, you'll need written documentation of the issues. Just like you'd do after a difficult face-to-face conversation, send an email summarizing what you talked about and the action items or next steps.

385

CREATE A CUSTOM SLACK EMOJI. These can help team jokes and norms stick, improve communication, and align the group. To upload a custom emoji to your company workspace, open Slack, click the emoji button in your text field, and click "Add Emoji." Next, select an image. For the best results, choose a fairly simple graphic or picture that'll be easy to interpret when it's shrunken down. Then, give it a name: ideally, something that's short, descriptive, and, of course, work-appropriate. (Don't forget that everyone in your workspace will be able to use this emoji!)

386

USE YOUR CUSTOM EMOJI TO HIGHLIGHT YOUR TEAM MEMBERS' VALUES. This is a fantastic use for custom emojis. Upload an emoji for each of your values. When a person on your team manifests one of your team values—like "Don't have an ego" or "Be curious"—react to their Slack message with the appropriate emoji. Your other reports will see the emoji, reinforcing the behavior across the team. You can also have people nominate their peers this way; essentially, each emoji counts as a vote. Each month or quarter, the person with the most votes for each value gets an award.

387

Consistently use this time to recognize
your team members for their hard work and accomplishments. You could end every all-hands meeting by asking if
anyone wants to recognize a coworker. Or if people are too
shy in the moment, you can ask them to send you their kudos
over chat or email before the meeting so you can read them
aloud. Whatever format you choose, this gives the entire team
an opportunity to cheer their peers on. It's a great morale
booster; plus, it helps you reinforce excellent performance.

388

MAKE A PERSONALIZED MESSAGE FOR DEPARTURES.
It's important to break the news anytime an employee leaves
the company, but it's critical when some or all of your team
is remote. Without a physical presence, the person who left
seems like they disappeared into thin air—which can breed
paranoia and insecurity among your remaining employees.
Combat this by sending a personalized team- or company-
wide email sharing the news. And even if the person isn't
leaving on good terms, make sure your email is respectful and
acknowledges the contributions they've made to the organization. For sensitive topics like this, you might need to go beyond
the usual email. Consider pairing your message with a recorded
video. Your employees will appreciate the human touch.

389

SHARE BIG NEWS OVER EMAIL. Because chat is typically more casual, it's not the first channel you should go to with significant announcements. And while you can and should mention relevant news during meetings, you also need something people can refer back to in the future. Email is the best fit for promotions, departures, internal job changes, company restructurings, and so on.

390

SCHEDULE YOUR OWN INFORMAL REVIEWS. If your company only does performance reviews once or twice a year, consider adding more frequent performance "check-ins." Nothing in your annual or biannual reviews should come as a surprise. In other words, every piece of feedback you give should have a precedent...which is where these informal reviews come in. Give your direct reports feedback whenever you have it (both positive and negative), taking notes along the way so you can pull the themes together for their performance review. One-on-ones are a good forum for this type of feedback. Alternatively, you can schedule "career conversations" every other month solely for professional development discussions.

391

HAVE YOUR TEAM MEMBERS UPDATE THEIR JOB DE-SCRIPTIONS. This exercise is a fantastic way to track your report's progress and make sure you're both measuring success by the same criteria. For example, perhaps their rewritten job description's "Responsibilities" section lists three low-value tasks and leaves out two critical ones. You can say, "Hey, you've included such and such, but I'd actually like you to (deprioritize, delegate, stop focusing on) those. I'd also like you to prioritize X and Y, which are essential for two reasons." Depending on how quickly your team members' jobs change, do this exercise every four to six months.

392

CREATE TRADITIONS THAT SPAN TIME ZONES. Just because a few of your employees are several hours ahead of (or behind) everyone else doesn't mean they should be left out of the team fun. Take a look at any existing rituals or recurring activities and ask yourself if they're friendly for all time zones. For example, do you have a monthly happy hour that's 5 p.m. for some people but 9 p.m. for others? The 9 p.m. folks probably aren't thrilled. Once you've reviewed your traditions, adapt them so everyone can participate. Instead of 5 p.m. cocktails, do noontime Bloody Marys and beers—the team members four hours ahead will appreciate it. And whenever you start a new tradition, make sure it's inclusive as well.

393

SET ASIDE A TRAVEL BUDGET. Every remote person on your team should have the opportunity to see their coworkers in person once per year, if not more. When you're planning the annual budget, make sure you have enough to finance these trips. And don't forget about yourself! As a manager, it's extra important for you to spend in-person time with your team members, as well as *your* boss, other managers, and company leadership.

394

PLAN A YEARLY TEAM RETREAT. Most remote and distributed teams say this annual trip is critical to their success. It gives everyone the opportunity to bond; brainstorm ideas; talk about the future of the department, company, and/or product; and more. Of course, between travel and accommodations, food and drinks, activities, and so on, retreats are a big expense—but the impact on your team's collaboration and work is incalculable.

395

When you're in the office, you have automatic visibility into how your team members work with others. But you're *not* in the office. To accurately and holistically evaluate their performance, you need to gather 360-degree feedback. Select three to eight people for each employee who can give you insight into their strengths and weaknesses. Try to pick people from a variety of other teams, if possible, to get the widest possible range of experiences. Then create a form with these three questions. Use the responses to identify core themes and then incorporate this feedback into your reports' performance reviews. You should run this exercise two or so times per year.

» What do you appreciate about working with (employee name) and what would you like them to continue doing?

» What would you like (employee name) to start doing? Please explain why, if it's not obvious.

» What would you like (employee name) to stop doing? Please include examples if possible.

HOW TO SUCCESSFULLY INTERVIEW AND HIRE THE BEST CANDIDATE VIRTUALLY

Hiring virtually? No problem! These hacks will help you make a strong impression during interviews *and* get a good sense of the candidate, even if you don't meet in person. Make interview and hiring processes feel a bit more manageable with guidance on how to find the best candidates and how to test their work-from-home aptitude.

396

CREATE A SHARED CHAT CHANNEL FOR INTERVIEWS.

Interviewing while working from home can be tricky—both for you and the interviewee. Technology issues are inevitable, scheduling conflicts are common, and virtual communication feels less intimate. For candidates that make it past the initial screening call, create a shared chat channel between the candidate and your interview panel. This makes it easy to coordinate interview dates and times; answer any questions they might have about the role, team, or company; share their resume, cover letter, and any other application materials with everyone at once; evaluate how well they write; and guide them through a skills assessment (like a live coding exercise or edit test).

397

ASK WFH-SPECIFIC INTERVIEW QUESTIONS. These questions should reveal the candidate's ability to work from home. Someone might have the right experience and skill set for the job, but if they haven't worked remotely before or don't have a compatible lifestyle, they might not be the best fit. To determine how well remote work will go for them, ask questions like the following:

» *"Imagine you need to give a team member some tough feedback. How would you deliver it in a remote environment?"* A good answer will reveal empathy and tact.
» *"What's your optimal communication cadence?"* Since remote work requires overcommunication, candidates who prefer infrequent communication might not be right for the role.
» *"How do you typically structure your day?"* Ideally, the candidate already has a system. If they don't, they may not be a fit for remote work.

398

POST YOUR JOB DESCRIPTION ON REMOTE WORK JOB SITES. The quality of applications is usually better than massive job boards; plus, you'll get candidates who are specifically looking for WFH roles. Check out We Work Remotely, Remote.co, and FlexJobs.

399

DO THE ENTIRE INTERVIEW PROCESS VIRTUALLY. You'll get valuable clues into the candidate's aptitude for remote work. Do they seem comfortable communicating over Skype or Zoom? When you give them interview dates and times, do they clarify the time zone? If you have technical issues mid-interview, can they calmly troubleshoot the issue? Any candidates who struggle during the interview process will *really* struggle working from home full time.

400

GIVE EVERY REMOTE CANDIDATE A WRITING TEST. It doesn't matter whether you're interviewing people for a job in HR, finance, customer service, marketing, sales, or engineering: *At least* 50 percent of their communication will be written. With that in mind, ask the candidates who make it past the first stage to write a blog post, tutorial, short memo, or even an email, depending on the job requirements. Do they make strong points? Do they include all the necessary information? Do their tone and style fit the situation? Is their writing clear and understandable? If you answer yes to all of these questions, this candidate has at least one of the traits they need to succeed in a remote environment.

401

ALWAYS BE RECRUITING (REMOTELY). Even though you're working from home, recruiting is probably an important part of your role. In fact, it might be even *more* important because you're no longer meeting potential candidates organically. To keep a full pipeline of people, schedule recruiting activities every month, such as external coffee dates, virtual conferences with networking opportunities, industry *Twitter* chats, calls with former colleagues, and so on. When the time comes to open up a role, you'll have plenty of contacts to reach out to.

. . .

402

FOCUS ON PROMOTING YOURSELF AND YOUR TEAM. As a remote employee, you're less visible. That's probably obvious. But what's less obvious? Everyone who reports to you is less visible too. Make sure you're equally, if not more, focused on sharing their accomplishments with the wider company and leadership as you are on sharing your own. When you talk about hitting a milestone, share the results of a successful experiment, discuss a new initiative your team is leading, and so on, cite the key people on your team who contributed. You'll look like an incredible manager, and they'll get a shout-out—everyone wins.

8 WAYS TO MANAGE NEW HIRES REMOTELY

It can be tricky starting a new job...and even trickier starting remotely! Not only must your new hire get up to speed with the various processes and tools you use, tackle their specific tasks and assignments, and meet their coworkers, but they might also need to establish a new WFH setup. Use these hacks to ease your new team member's transition.

403

CREATE A WFH QUESTIONNAIRE. This is an easy way to ask new hires about their WFH setup and ensure they have everything they need. Is their Internet connection strong enough? Do they have somewhere comfortable and reasonably quiet to sit and work? Will they need any additional gear, like a headset, monitor, or desk chair? Is there any software they should install before day one? If you're expecting them to provide their own computer, do they have one that'll work? You want to find out sooner rather than later if there's something that'll impede their productivity, and having a premade list can make this a lot easier for both of you.

404

GIVE EACH NEW HIRE A MENTOR. Assigning an experienced employee to guide a new team member through their first several months is valuable no matter what: They can answer questions the new hire might be self-conscious about asking others, fill them in on any unwritten norms, and point them toward additional resources as problems come up. Mentors are especially important if you are working remotely and/or the new hire is remote. Since you don't have an in-person connection with your report, you need to give them extra support.

405

CREATE A 30-60-90-DAY PLAN FOR NEW HIRES. A 30-60-90 plan maps out what your employee should focus on learning and achieving within their first, second, and third month on the job. It's a helpful resource for all new hires, but it's particularly helpful for distributed teams. The physical distance between you and your report can make them feel slightly adrift or isolated—having clear, time-based goals will make them feel connected to you, the team, and the rest of the company and reassure them they're focusing on the right things.

406

MAKE YOUR NEW HIRE'S FIRST DAY FEEL SPECIAL BY SENDING THEM A WELCOME PACKAGE. Without a new office, a new workspace, or new coworkers beside them, starting a new remote job can feel anticlimactic. A package of goodies will make all the difference. In your welcome box, include company swag, coffee and a mug, snacks, and a note saying you're excited to have them on board.

407

DELEGATE PARTS OF THE ONBOARDING EXPERIENCE. Without random interactions in the office, new remote employees often find it harder to get to know the rest of the team. Having members of your team own individual parts of onboarding will give your new hire a chance to meet the others early on. You might ask one employee to walk them through your team's tech stack, another to explain how goals are tracked and reported, another to give a rundown of your project management system, and so on. By the end of onboarding, your new employee will feel fully in the loop.

408

CHECK IN MORE FREQUENTLY. Your more established coworkers can probably tackle most, if not all, of their work on their own. Your new hires, however, might appreciate a little more attention—especially when one or both of you is working from home. Touching base with them over chat, phone, or video every two or three days, rather than once every week or two weeks, will give them a chance to bring up any questions or concerns on their mind. More importantly, it will demonstrate that even though you're not in the same place, you're still very much around.

409

CREATE AN ONBOARDING CHECKLIST FOR NEW HIRES. This checklist should cover everything they should do to get set up successfully in their first few months, from personalizing their email signature and familiarizing themselves with the team's communication protocols to completing paperwork and filling out the new team member questionnaire. This checklist will make onboarding less overwhelming for your employees—and more structured and efficient for you.

410

PLAN A REMOTE LUNCH OR DRINKS. To help your new employee feel connected to the rest of the team from the get-go, do something celebratory with the team. You can't take them out for a meal, but you *can* send everyone gift cards to a food delivery service—or instructions to expense a bottle of wine or six-pack of beer. (This is also a great idea for other exciting events or celebrations. You can even use it as a morale booster for a team that's been working hard.)

• • •

411

KEEP YOUR TEAM'S TIME ZONES SOMEWHERE YOU CAN EASILY REFERENCE. Like a "notepad" saved to your computer desktop, a Word doc that you can pull up at any time, or even a paper pinned up next to your desk. Check this list when you're scheduling meetings or sending messages at an off-hour time so you can avoid booking or pinging someone when they're offline. This hack is especially effective if you work with people from a lot of different time zones so you can easily see who's working where at any time.

412

KEEP TRACK OF HOW MUCH VACATION TIME EACH PERSON HAS TAKEN. If people aren't using enough out-of-office time, they may be overwhelmed with work. Or they might be more hesitant to take time off if they've just started a new WFH routine. They're also probably approaching burn-out. Talk to the team members who haven't taken enough (or any) time off and gently encourage them to schedule a break.

413

SET YOUR TEAM'S CORE HOURS. Core hours (or a block of time, like 10 a.m. to 2 p.m., during which you're always online) are important for working collaboratively with others. It's helpful to set team-wide core hours so that there's one period per day that everyone can get a quick response, schedule meetings, and "hang out" together on chat. Look at your team's various time zones. Is there a range of one to five hours where everyone overlaps? If so, you've found your core hours. Tell your team they should try to be online and available during this period as much as possible; they can work whenever they'd like outside these hours. But, of course, be flexible. If someone needs to log off from 1 to 2 p.m. each day for a family obligation, let them.

414

SET UP SLACKBOT TO MONITOR FOR NON-INCLUSIVE LANGUAGE. Encouraging your team to use inclusive phrases can have a huge impact on how comfortable people feel bringing their whole selves to work. But stepping in every time someone says, "Hey guys" or "That's insane" is a full-time job. Luckily, you can customize your workplace's Slackbot to respond to custom words and terms—putting your "inclusivity filter" on autopilot. For example, when someone says, "Hey guys," have Slackbot say, "What about a gender-neutral term like 'folks,' 'everyone,' 'squad,' 'crew,' 'y'all,' or 'team'?" When someone says, "insane" or "crazy," have Slackbot say, "Using 'insane' or 'crazy' can marginalize people suffering from mental illness. What about 'unbelievable,' 'impressive,' 'ridiculous,' or 'unprecedented'?"

415

COMMUNICATE IMPORTANT THINGS THREE TIMES IN THREE DIFFERENT WAYS. For example, if you're sharing next year's goals, talk about them in the team meeting, share them over email, and post a link to your dashboard over chat. "Three times, three ways" might feel like overkill, but it's critical to keep everyone on the same page. Say one employee missed the team meeting but saw the email and Slack message. They'll still be up to date.

416

STANDARDIZE FOLDER STRUCTURE AND FILE NAMES TO MAKE FINDING AND SHARING INFORMATION EASIER. The bigger and older your team is, the more information you have to keep track of. This task gets a lot harder when people give their files obscure, vague, or random names, like "Analysis Summer." Create a team-wide structure for folders and files. For example, maybe you have three main folders for each type of project, which are divided into folders by year. Each file is named using a specific format, like "[Client Name]-[Date]." Once you have a system, it doesn't matter who created or last updated a file—it'll be easy to dig up.

417

SHARE YOUR PRIORITIES WITH YOUR TEAM SO THEY FEEL ENGAGED AND MOTIVATED. The more insight they have into your goals, the more responsible they'll feel for helping achieve those goals. Consider posting your priorities for the week on chat, sending an email every Friday recapping your progress and setting your goals for the next week, or discussing what you're working toward during your daily stand-up or team meeting.

418

KEEP YOUR TO-DO LIST UNDER CONTROL WITH THE FOUR-MINUTE RULE. Here's how it works: Every time a new task pops up that'll take you less than four minutes, do it immediately. This is faster than adding it to your to-do list and returning to it later or, worse, not writing it down and thinking about the work all day. (Of course, you have to balance this by silencing notifications and other distractions when you want to focus; otherwise, you'll be doing "four-minute tasks" all day long.)

419

ASK YOUR TEAM TO RESEND ANY IMPORTANT MESSAGES. Losing control of your inbox isn't ideal, but it happens. Say you don't have enough time right now to go through tons of unread messages, and you're worried important questions or updates are falling through the cracks. The solution is simple (and your team will appreciate the transparency). Say, "Hey, everyone, I need your help. My inbox has run away from me. If there's anything you need me to answer within the next few days, can you please resend it and put 'Timely' in the subject line?"

420

TAKE OVER YOUR REPORTS' SCREENS FOR DEMOS.
Let's say you're walking your report through using a database, helping them debug an issue in a customer account, or providing feedback on their wireframes. Rather than giving them instructions and watching their mouse flail around, request control of their screen so you can show them how to do it. To enable this on Zoom, have your team member share their screen. Find the screen-sharing toolbar and click "Request Remote Control." If you're using GoToMeeting, ask your report to open their control panel, click the arrow next to your name, and select "Make presenter." Using Google Meet? Your employee needs to install Chrome Remote Desktop. Once it's downloaded, they can generate a code that'll let you take over their computer.

421

HOST REGULAR ACTIVITIES TO BOOST TEAM MORALE.
Since your team can't go out for drinks after work, catch up in the hallways, or eat lunch together, they won't be as close as a traditional team. At least, not without some effort on your part. Scheduling a virtual team get-together will give your team valuable bonding time. Consider setting up a team lunch during the day or a "happy hour" once your core hours are over. Once a month is a good cadence—especially because remote activities are typically shorter than in-person ones.

422

SEND OUT A MONTHLY OR QUARTERLY NEWSLETTER ABOUT YOUR TEAM. Share nonwork-related info about your team, like birthdays, anniversaries, pictures, and videos from team and company events; personal news that anyone's opted to share; and even trivia about your team members, such as "Did you know Jane Doe won a world yodeling competition?" The newsletter will give everyone talking points in meetings, help them bring their full selves to work, and ultimately make your team feel closer and more connected.

423

SUBSCRIBE TO NEWS UPDATES FROM AROUND THE WORLD. It might be a slow news week where *you* live, but something major might be happening in your employee's country. Keeping up with the major stories in their area will give you the heads-up when you need to check in. If something noteworthy or important happens, ask how they're doing. They may say, "Thanks, I'm completely fine!" or "Actually, I'm glad you brought that up. I'm really struggling." Either way, you will show that you care and are open to discussing these topics.

424

SHARE A LIST OF KEY INTERNAL CONTACTS WITH YOUR TEAM. This list will help you avoid getting pinged with IT, finance, and HR requests. It should include every person your employees may need to contact for questions outside your scope, like hardware/software issues, VPN access, username and password changes, paychecks, taxes, expense reimbursements, benefits, and more.

425

CREATE A CAREER LADDER SO YOUR TEAM MEMBERS HAVE CLEAR GOALS TO WORK TOWARD. A career ladder is a plan that lays out a typical employee's role progression by responsibilities, performance, and tier. It's highly motivating for employees, especially remote ones, because it demystifies the promotion process and gives them an objective framework for measuring their progress. Career ladders are common in engineering and sales, but can be used for all departments.

426

USE A SYSTEM FOR NAMING CHAT CHANNELS SO IT'S EASY TO JOIN THE RIGHT ONES. Channel names should be descriptive, unique, and standardized, like [Team Name Abbreviation]-[Interior or Exterior Abbreviation]-[Purpose]. For instance, if you manage the Customer Success team, a channel you share with Product Marketing would be #cs-ext-product-mktg-sync, whereas a team channel for discussing your pets would be #cs-int-pet-talk.

427

FOSTER COLLABORATION AND CONTINUAL LEARNING WITH LUNCH-AND-LEARNS. Virtual lunch-and-learns expose your team to new points of view, expertise, or experience. Ask the leader of another department to walk everyone through their team's goals, operations, and challenges, or bring in someone external to talk about their career, day-to-day work, and any advice they might have. Because these events are typically held during lunchtime, they're definitely not mandatory. However, your employees might find them helpful, so try scheduling a monthly or quarterly lunch-and-learn to gauge interest.

428

BUILD TRANSPARENCY AND TRUST WITH TEAM- OR COMPANY-WIDE ASK-ME-ANYTHING (AMA) SESSIONS.
Have employees send in their questions anonymously, and then set up a presentation or large-group meeting to share the answers. Although these can be especially reassuring or informative during transition periods, they're helpful for assessing employee satisfaction at any time. For example, maybe you're getting a lot of questions about the future of the department or your multiyear plan. That tells you employees are excited about where the company is going or need more clarity on how their work fits into the larger vision. Or perhaps you start seeing more questions than usual about compensation and benefits—a clue that some team members might be feeling underpaid.

429

BRING YOUR KIDS (OR FUR KIDS) TO WORK. Next time your child or pet runs into the room while you're on a video call, don't panic and try to get them off-screen as soon as possible. Bring them onto your lap or turn the camera so they can wave to the meeting participants. Showing your team that it's okay if life sometimes interrupts work will make them feel a lot more comfortable if their kid or pet barges in too. Not to mention, you'll come across as relatable and human.

430

GET CREATIVE WHEN PICKING OUT EMPLOYEE PERKS.
You can't reward remote employees with parking spots, corner offices, or bagels and coffee. But don't cut this line item from your budget completely. Perks are a cornerstone of employee retention *and* recruiting. Consider paying for your WFH team members' office equipment; giving them a monthly "healthy living" credit for gym memberships, yoga classes, workout gear, and so on; a snack box subscription; and/or tuition reimbursement.

CHAPTER 7

MAINTAINING YOUR WORK-LIFE BALANCE

431

LIST YOUR LIFE PRIORITIES. Don't try to get *everything* done, or you'll quickly burn out. Instead, figure out your essentials—both professional and personal—and rank them. Maybe that's spending time with your family, followed by doing well at work, followed by exercising four times a week. Or maybe it's getting a promotion, then learning to code, then gardening. Whatever your priorities are, use them to organize your to-do list—and figure out the things you can cut.

432

SET AN ALARM FOR THE END OF YOUR WORKDAY. Commit to powering down your computer when that alarm goes off. Start wrapping up everything you're doing at least half an hour before the alarm is set to ring so you don't have to log off mid-task. After you've used this strategy for a few weeks, you'll automatically sense when it's your stopping time.

433

WORK FROM A LOCATION THAT CLOSES AROUND YOUR QUITTING TIME. Maybe that's a coffee shop that's open until 2 p.m. or the library that closes at 6 p.m. This gives you a built-in end time. You'll also have a quasi-commute from wherever you're working to your home, the gym, or wherever you're heading next.

434

COMMIT TO A WORK-LIFE BALANCE GOAL. Spending too much time on work and not enough on life? Consider setting a specific goal to help you find the right balance. To increase your likelihood of following through, commit to one goal at a time, and make sure it's a SMART one: specific, measurable, achievable, realistic, and timely. A non-SMART goal would be "I'll stop working so much." The SMART version: "I'll log off before 6:30 p.m. at least three nights per week for the next month."

435

MAKE PLANS AFTER WORK. To hold yourself accountable to a stopping time, pencil in plans with a friend or family member. Those might be in person, like dinner or drinks, or virtual, like FaceTime-ing each other while you watch your favorite show. Add these plans to your calendar so they feel legitimate.

436

DEDICATE ONE OR TWO NIGHTS A WEEK TO A RECURRING ACTIVITY. Maybe that's taking a workout class you really enjoy, joining a local bowling league, or simply deciding that every Wednesday evening is officially "Cook a Fancy Dinner Night." Committing to doing the same thing on the same day every week automates the "life" part of work-life balance. This also makes it easier to coordinate activities with friends, since you don't have to worry about finding a time you're both free.

437

SCHEDULE ALONE TIME. Since you see fewer people in person than an office employee, you might be tempted to fill up every evening with a different social activity. But even the most extreme extroverts need time by themselves. Block out at least one or two nights per week for yourself—whether you're going for a solo dinner, hopping in the tub with a drink and a book, taking a long walk, spending your time on a hobby, or even running errands. Anything that calms you down and gives you some space will do the trick.

438

SET YOURSELF TO "AWAY." The best way to stay out of your inbox when you're not working? Turn off your email notifications and set your chat status to "away." If you don't see the messages pop up, you won't be tempted to read them. In Slack, this mode is called "Do Not Disturb" or "DND." Handily, your coworkers can choose to override "DND" and send you a message notification if it's urgent. In Microsoft Teams, this is also called "Do Not Disturb." In Google Hangouts, you can simply mute notifications for as long as you're logged off.

439

SPLIT YOUR TO-DO LIST INTO "PERSONAL" AND "PRO-FESSIONAL." Some remote workers love the ability to balance household duties with their professional ones, while others find it impossible to get both done. If you like doing chores during your work breaks, add them to a separate section of your to-do list. This helps you switch more seamlessly between your personal and professional tasks and creates a stronger separation between the two parts of your life.

440

GIVE YOURSELF AN APP-FREE CHALLENGE. You probably won't read and respond to emails, *LinkedIn* invites, or chat messages when it's not convenient. If you have the app on your phone, you might be tempted to check on things at all hours of the day and night. It's a lot less likely that you'll pause your show, get up off the couch, head to your office, and start up your computer to check your work email. So select the apps you use most for work and challenge yourself to delete these apps for just a day or two. If this goes well, challenge yourself to delete them for a week. After you've successfully done this challenge a few times, you'll feel more comfortable keeping email, chat, and more off your phone permanently.

441

SCHEDULE NOTIFICATIONS TO START AND STOP WITH YOUR WORK HOURS. To make it even harder to check your chat at night or right when you wake up, schedule notifications for 9 a.m. to 6 p.m. (or whatever your working hours are). If you're using Slack, look for the "notification schedule" option in the menu; in Microsoft Teams, this feature is called "Quiet Hours." Now you won't see any notifications outside those hours, even when people email or message you.

442

DON'T SHARE YOUR CELL PHONE NUMBER. With all the communication tools at our disposal, your team or boss shouldn't need your number. Don't open the door for after-hours calls or texts. The only exception is if your manager explicitly asks you for your cell or there's an expectation at the company you'll be available at any time.

443

GET A WORK PHONE. If you do work in a role that requires constant availability, see if your company will pay for a phone. Having a separate phone creates some psychological space. Plus, it means you won't see work-related notifications pop up when you're scrolling through social media in the evening or taking photos on the weekend.

444

CUSTOMIZE YOUR NOTIFICATIONS. If you're not ready to turn off notifications completely, limit the number you receive so interruptions are few and far between. You can find the sweet spot by identifying which types of notifications you need to see no matter what and filtering everything *but* those. For example, you could turn off all notifications but direct messages and mentions of "product failure" or "product emergency." Or maybe you want to mute notifications for a channel that's particularly chatty. Figure out what works for you.

445

TRACK HOW MUCH PERSONAL TIME YOU SPEND DO-ING WORK ON YOUR PHONE. It might surprise you. To see just how many minutes (hours!) you're spending each day on email, *LinkedIn*, chat, and so on, open Screen Time (iOS) or Digital Wellbeing (Android). Tally up the professional app usage—then add that amount of time to the hours you already put in each day. If you're pushing nine-plus hours, it's time to set stricter boundaries.

446

SET TIME LIMITS ON WORK APPS. If you're not ready to purge work-related tools from your phone, curtail your usage of them. iOS users can do this in Screen Time, which allows you to cap how many minutes or hours per day you can have a specific app open. Reached the limit? Apple gives you the option to "snooze" (use the app for fifteen more minutes) or ignore that day's limit entirely. Android users have Digital Wellbeing—a suite of tools that let you set specific app time limits. Beware, because once you've used up all your time, you can't get any more.

447

DON'T SLEEP WITH YOUR PHONE BY YOUR BED. Does this sound familiar? You wake up, you pick up your phone to see what time it is, you see an email notification, so you read it—and the next thing you know, you're three messages deep and fully alert at 5:45 a.m. Protect your sleep by keeping your phone in a separate room...or at least across the room. Get a clock for your bedside table instead.

448

ENABLE AIRPLANE MODE AT NIGHT. Then turn off your Wi-Fi. This two-step hack will limit all notifications and keep you from browsing the Internet or using Internet-reliant apps while still giving you access to your camera, photos, flashlight, and calculator. You'll also be able to read ebooks or listen to podcasts that you've previously downloaded to your phone. Challenge yourself to keep airplane mode on until you've been up for at least forty-five minutes.

449

DON'T WFB (WORK FROM BED). Lying back on your pillows while you type might be comfortable, but it'll throw your work-life balance out of whack. You need to set clear boundaries between "work" and "life," or you'll feel like you're always stuck between the two. Doing *anything* in bed that's not sleeping can also make it harder to fall asleep at night, since it confuses your brain about what your bed is for.

450

GIVE YOURSELF PLENTY OF TIME TO START THE DAY. Nothing is stopping you from waking up, dashing out of bed, gulping some coffee, and starting your workday. Unfortunately, this habit is horrible for your work-life balance. Give yourself plenty of time to settle into your workday so that there's a clear distinction between sleep and work.

451

GIVE YOURSELF TIME TO WIND DOWN BEFORE BED SO YOU CAN ACTUALLY REST. If you're sending out a few more emails right before you turn off your light and go to sleep, it'll feel like there's no separation between work and the rest of your life. On top of that, the artificial blue light from your phone or computer messes with your body's internal clock—making it harder to enter dreamland. The National Sleep Foundation recommends ending your screen time thirty minutes to two hours before your bedtime, so use that guideline when figuring out when your workday should end. Take some time to check out from work, engage in a hobby you enjoy, and give yourself some downtime before heading to bed.

452

MATCH YOUR CALENDAR WORKING HOURS TO YOUR SCHEDULE. Most calendar and scheduling apps, including Google Calendar, Microsoft Outlook, and Calendly, let you set custom working hours. If someone tries to book you outside of these, it'll ask them if they're sure (or, for some tools, block them from creating a meeting altogether). This is another great tool for making sure you protect your early-morning and evening hours so you get the time you need to relax.

453

GUARD YOUR MORNINGS AND EVENINGS BY MAKING YOUR TIME ZONE CLEAR. Work with people around the nation or even the world? Make it easy for them to identify your time zone so they don't try to schedule you for meetings or calls when you're not available. One option is to put your time zone in your profile. This will discourage messages from your coworkers when it's early or late where you live. To make things as easy as possible, you can even do the math for them. For example, if most of your team lives in Dublin but you're in New York, your status should be something like "East Coast: five hours behind Dublin." When they see you're in a different time zone, they'll typically email you instead. Or block off the time you'd ideally like to be unavailable on your calendar. For instance, you can block off 7 p.m. to 9 a.m. your time with the title "I'm on [time zone]—please don't book unless it's urgent!"

454

SET A RECURRING REMINDER TO TAKE VACATION TIME. To hold yourself accountable to getting out of the office, create a monthly or quarterly reminder. You can do this in a task manager tool or create an event on your calendar. Label the reminder or event something like "Have you scheduled any time off since last (month, quarter)?"

455

DECLINE INVITATIONS FOR MEETINGS HAPPENING WHILE YOU'RE OUT. Once you've scheduled your out-of-office time on Google Calendar, it will automatically RSVP "no" to all existing and new invitations scheduled during that time. Outlook doesn't have the same feature, but there's a workaround. Add all of your direct team members to an all-day event that corresponds with your vacation dates and label it "(Your name) OOO." Make sure the "Show As" setting is "free," or this time will be blocked on your coworkers' calendars.

456

DON'T TAKE YOUR WORK ON VACATION. That means no answering emails, reading chats, or opening updates on the internal wiki. You might feel like you're proving your dedication to your company by sending out a few quick responses while you're out of the office, but you're actually pulling yourself out of your vacation—so you'll feel less rejuvenated when it's over. You're also setting a bad example for your colleagues and anyone who might report to you. If you don't give yourself the time off, they won't feel comfortable doing so either.

457

GET AN OUT-OF-OFFICE BUDDY. Establish who will keep track of different tasks, assignments, and requests while you're out of the office. Then, in your automated out-of-office reply, you can let people know which coworker is fielding requests until you're back. This way, if something urgent comes up, you're far less likely to get a panicked text or email; your teammate can step in. You'll also have fewer messages to tackle when your vacation is over. Depending on what your role is, ask your peer or boss for their help. You can also give different tasks to different people, such as "For questions on hiring, please talk to Kenia; for anything else, please talk to Finn." Don't forget to ask for your colleagues' permission before you name them in the email.

458

REQUEST SPECIFIC SUBJECT LINES. Worried about missing urgent emails while on vacation? In your away email, ask people to put "urgent" in the subject line for anything that can't wait until your return. Create a filter for emails with "urgent" in the subject line. You can quickly log in to your inbox, make sure the "urgent" folder is still empty, and log back out. Only use this strategy if you're confident it won't be abused and that you actually might need to step in to resolve a time-sensitive issue.

459

BUILD BUFFER DAYS INTO YOUR VACATION. Going right back to work can shatter any sense of calm you've cultivated as you rush to get everything back in order at home when you return. It also makes any travel delays super stressful—as your plane's departure gets pushed back, then back again, all you're thinking about is how little sleep you're going to get that night. Save yourself from this fate by coming home a day early or adding an additional day to your out-of-office time. You can use this day to get reacclimated to your normal schedule, unpack, do laundry, meal prep, catch up on emails, and so on...so when you head back to the virtual office, you still feel refreshed.

460

ADOPT SUMMER FRIDAYS. As the sun comes out, work tends to cool off—for some industries, at least. Consider implementing Summer Fridays at your team or company. Every Friday, folks log off at noon. While you'll lose five or six hours of work, the boost in morale means more gets done. And if you don't have the power to make this change yourself, suggest it to someone who can!

461

GIVE YOURSELF A VACATION MINIMUM. Perfect for people with unlimited paid time off, it's important to make a commitment to yourself to take at least twenty vacation days per year. Surprisingly, when people can take as much time off as they'd like, they typically end up taking less. A personal vacation minimum will ensure you don't short yourself on valuable R and R time.

462

FIND NEW COMMUNITIES ON SLACK. While Slack is usually considered a tool for work communication, it can actually be a great way to explore other hobbies or interests. Network, chat about your passions or causes, and get a sense of belonging by joining special interest Slack groups. Take a look at your company's channels; you'll probably find several devoted to nonwork topics like reading, gardening, cycling, cooking, even home brewing. If you're a freelancer, there are plenty of public special interest groups out there as well. Just Google "Slack group [insert passion here]" and see what comes up. And if you don't find a group you're interested in, create one! Chances are, if you're interested in it, other people are too. Don't forget to post a brief plug for it in relevant channels— for instance, if you're starting a #starwars channel, you should let the folks in #movies and #off-topic know.

463

USE THE BURNOUT INDEX TO GAUGE YOUR MENTAL HEALTH. This two-minute online test is based on psychological assessments and helps you measure your risk of burning out. Take it every month or so and record your results in a spreadsheet or notebook. If you start to slide into burnout, you'll be able to catch the signs early.

464

MAKE USE OF A MEAL KIT DELIVERY SERVICE. Working from home means having your favorite snacks just a few steps away. But it's easy to go overboard. To ensure you're still getting enough healthy, homemade food, subscribe to a meal kit delivery service. You can get everything you need to cook delicious meals delivered right to your doorstep at the frequency you choose. Skip the trip to the grocery store, hours of prep time in the kitchen, and last-minute substitutions because you forgot to buy coriander or baking soda. All you need to do is open the box, take out your ingredients, and follow the kit's instructions to whip up a nutritious and tasty meal.

465

USE A RANDOM PAIRING APP TO CONNECT WITH PEOPLE FOR LUNCH. Often find yourself working through your lunch break? Apps like Donut let you set up a "lunch roulette" system. Every week or month (depending on the cadence you choose), participants will get introduced to a randomly selected buddy from within the company for a coffee chat or lunch. It's a great way to meet people you might not otherwise, and gives you an excuse to disconnect from your work for a little bit.

466

MULTITASK WITH AN UNDER-THE-DESK ELLIPTICAL OR CYCLE. Can't find a spare minute to work out? Thanks to ellipticals and bike-pedal equipment that go under your desk, you can exercise and work at the same time. Some users rack up ten to twenty miles every day. Under-desk ellipticals and cycles typically range in price from $50 to $200. Look for one that'll fit into your space, will stay put on the floor, and won't make much noise. But don't take any meetings while you're working out: Heavy breathing and sweatiness aren't just distracting; they're also unprofessional.

467

LOG OFF ON THE WEEKENDS. Firmly delineating "work time" from "personal time" is even more critical for remote workers, since technically you can work at any time. To keep yourself from slipping, put your work laptop on a high shelf or in a drawer on Friday night. Don't touch it until Monday morning.

468

SCHEDULE TIME FOR EXERCISE. You tend to move less when you're working from home, since you're staying in one place all day. Block out thirty minutes to an hour for exercising on your calendar to ensure your physical health doesn't fall by the wayside. If possible, work out at a time you typically feel listless. It might sound counterintuitive, but any physical activity that raises your heart rate will increase your energy.

469

CONNECT WITH FRIENDS IN ALL DIFFERENT PLACES WITH A VIRTUAL COOKBOOK CLUB. This is a fun way to spend time with people who are too far away for in-person visits. Organize a small to medium group (six is a good number for keeping the conversation manageable). Vote on a new cookbook each month and prepare a meal to bring to your virtual dinner—or choose a different recipe from the same cookbook each time so everyone can compare notes on how it turned out.

470

PRACTICE A CRAFT OUTSIDE YOUR HOME. Give yourself a reason to get out of the house once the clock strikes five: Find a local pottery, glassmaking, or art studio and see if they offer classes or workshops. A hobby will help you disconnect from work—especially if you're going from a mental activity to a hands-on one. And if you've made a financial commitment, you're likelier to keep going.

471

DO THINGS HALFWAY. If you're having trouble fitting exercise, socializing, self-care, and the like into your schedule, make those activities shorter. For instance, maybe you're used to hitting the gym for an hour, but lately you haven't had the time. Rather than skipping a workout entirely, go for just twenty minutes. Call your friend while you walk around your neighborhood if you can't swing a two-hour dinner date. Wash just the dishes in your sink if you can't tackle the entire kitchen. Compromising will help you do more in the same amount of time.

472

HIRE A PRIVATE INSTRUCTOR. You can find a teacher in your area for almost any skill under the sun: pizza making, roller-blading, guitar playing, floral arranging, sewing, and so on. And now that your commute is seconds long, you have more time for a hobby. If you're watching your wallet, try a group course instead.

473

DON'T SHOW WEEKENDS ON YOUR CALENDAR. To help yourself log off, hide weekends in your calendar tool. That way, you'll have no reason to look at your schedule on the weekends. Set this up in Google Calendar by clicking the time period (next to the settings icon) and unchecking "Show weekends." Set this up in Apple Calendar by clicking "Week" (at the top of the window) and then "Show 5."

474

MULTITASK WITH CALL RECORDINGS. Couldn't make a meeting and need to catch up? This could be a great time to get some household chores done. Try playing the recording during tasks you can do on semi-autopilot—like folding laundry, washing dishes, or weeding—instead of listening to a podcast or music.

475

GET A DOG. Having a walk-loving animal on your hands is a great way to guarantee you get outside multiple times a day. A dog will also keep you company on long WFH days. If you didn't get a pet as a traditional office worker because you were worried about leaving them alone all day...problem solved.

476

SCHEDULE TIME FOR WALKING AND PLAYING WITH YOUR PET. To ensure you get in all the face time with your cat, dog, or other creature that you need (hey, they're an important stakeholder!), block out time on your calendar for taking them for walks or simply snuggling. You won't feel as guilty ignoring their cute face when you know you've got dedicated playtime coming up in an hour.

477

RUN ONE ERRAND PER DAY. This habit will help you keep your to-do list in check—but more importantly, it'll give you a reason to get dressed every day and leave the house. You'll also get some fresh air and social interaction. If you don't have five-plus errands to run a week, give yourself a treat and stop for a snack or browse a store of your choice without a specific goal in mind.

478

STOP KEEPING COFFEE AT HOME. Need more incentive to actually get up and get dressed in the morning? Let yourself run out of coffee at home. Each morning, you'll have to head to a coffee shop if you want your caffeine fix. This might sound extreme, but try it for a few days and see if your mood, productivity, and mental health benefit from a daily excursion.

479

REVIEW YOUR WORK-LIFE BALANCE WITH YOUR MANAGER. Clocking a fifty-, sixty-, or even seventy-hour week isn't fun—especially if it's not the first week you've worked overtime. So check in with your manager to figure out how to establish a better balance. Let them know that you have a lot on your plate and are worried about the quality of your work. Once you give them some details about your workload, they should be able to help you figure out what to prioritize and what can be put to the side. This exercise will let you get done what you need to without burning yourself out. (It's worth noting that in many industries, work ebbs and flows. Keep this in mind when you tap in your boss—this conversation won't go well if, say, you're an accountant and it's tax season.)

It's easier to stick to your goals when you're working toward them with others—and who better to focus on work-life balance with you than your team members? You can truly hold one another accountable; after all, you'll know if they're sending emails over the weekend or working while "out of the office." Even better, when several people on a team are practicing good work-life balance habits, the rest of the team usually follows suit. If you don't get emails on the weekend, you won't *respond* to emails on the weekend. After a while, you'll stop checking your inbox from Friday evening until Monday morning. To improve your team's collective work-life balance, try these ideas.

480

TAKE A COLLECTIVE VOLUNTEER DAY. Working together to support a cause you care about can be a great way to connect with your coworkers outside the office. And if you're not able to meet in person, consider virtual options so everyone has the opportunity to participate. If it's not feasible to all take the same day off, petition your employer to give everyone a paid volunteer day per year.

481

DO WALKING ONE-ON-ONES. An easy way to squeeze in some extra exercise and get away from your desk? Call your coworkers on the phone and take a walk while you talk. Of course, you'll need to make sure you don't need access to your computer or notes while you're walking, but this method is perfect for lighter, easier catch-ups when you're not addressing any pressing issues.

482

COMMIT TO A GROUP GOAL. Is there a change you all want to make, like exercising at least three times per week, eating lunch away from your desk for a month, or reading one new book a month? Tackle it as a team by taking a short group walk in the afternoon, agreeing to meet in the lunchroom at a certain time every day, or starting a book club.

483

HOST A REMOTE "TALENT SHOW." Show how much you appreciate and value your coworkers' hobbies! Host a virtual talent show where people can show off their musical skills, demonstrate a new dance routine from their ballroom dancing classes, or even read aloud something they wrote. To make it family-friendly, invite your team to get their kids in on the act.

484

ENCOURAGE PEOPLE TO SHARE PICTURES OF THEIR LIVES. Whether it's pictures of their pets, kids, or even baking projects, you want people to feel comfortable sharing whatever is important to them. Use a different prompt each week so everyone can participate. Get to know one another as whole people outside your tasks within the office.

485

DON'T FORGET TO CELEBRATE. Hit a big work milestone? Celebrating a birthday? Throwing a work-friendly bridal or baby shower? Take a break from working to have a virtual party. Send out food delivery service gift cards, have everyone order their food beforehand, and have a video call while you eat and hang out. And, if you need a group card, use platforms like Open Me and Group Greeting, which let you pick out a card style, add text and photos, send the link to everyone who needs to sign it, and then deliver it to the recipient at your preferred date and time. It's a fun way to celebrate birthdays, work anniversaries, pregnancy announcements, role changes, new jobs, and more.

486

RUN A RACE "TOGETHER." Have everyone sign up for a local 5K—or simply plan to run or walk a 5K wherever they are on your pre-chosen race day. Create a chat channel so people can share their finish times and race pictures.

. . .

487

PUT YOUR TRASH CAN IN A DIFFERENT ROOM. Every time you need to throw something away, you'll be forced to get up and walk around a bit. It's a great way to build small breaks into your workday and keep yourself from sitting too long. If you rarely need to use a trash can, try the same hack but with your phone.

488

TAKE THAT SICK TIME. Just because you don't have to worry about passing on your bug to your coworkers doesn't mean you should tough your way through it. A good rule of thumb: If you'd be too sick to go to the office, you're too sick to work from home. When you're under the weather, your work quality will be mediocre at best. You'll also increase your risk of burning out.

489

THINK OF YOURSELF AS A CONSULTANT WHO BILLS BY THE PROJECT, NOT THE HOUR. If you're hyper-focused on making sure you're working exactly eight hours a day—especially if you're at the point where you're tracking the minutes you spend working—you might need to readjust your thinking. Think of your work based on projects, not time. This mindset forces you to think about how much value you're creating, instead of how much time you're logging. It will lessen any guilt or anxiety you might feel around taking vacation, logging off early, or having a quiet day.

490

MOTIVATE YOURSELF TO MAKE HEALTHY CHOICES WITH A HABIT-TRACKING TOOL. Apps like Strides (iOS), Done (iOS), and Loop Habit Tracker (Android) let you set goals (like "spend more time on my hobbies") and habits (such as "go to bed before 11 p.m. every night") and then log whether you were successful. Both apps come with easy-to-use charts to help you monitor your progress and learn more about what helps you meet your goals. You can even set reminders to keep yourself on track.

11 WORK-LIFE BALANCE TIPS FOR FREELANCERS

Working for yourself can be incredibly fulfilling, exciting, and even lucrative—yet one thing it's typically *not*? Balanced. To an outsider, it might seem like you have no boss, but that's actually not the case. On the contrary, you have a ton: Every client is essentially your boss. That can quickly lead to over-lapping deadlines; calls, messages, and texts at every time of day and night; different work styles; and more. In addition, since your income hinges on your output, you probably struggle to stop working when you need a break—let alone say no to new jobs or take days off. That doesn't mean finding work-life balance as a freelancer is impossible. If you're intentional about when, where, and how you work, you can achieve it. These eleven hacks will go a long way toward helping you.

491

BAKE BUFFER TIME INTO YOUR TIMELINE ESTIMATES.
Depending on the project's scope, add a day to a few weeks to the deadline you agree on with the client. If anything takes longer than you anticipate, there will be no need to stress—you'll still finish on time. And if you don't use the buffer time and finish "early"? Your client will be thrilled.

492

COMBAT "SCOPE CREEP" BY NEVER TAKING A JOB WITHOUT A COMPREHENSIVE CONTRACT. Your agreement should lay out what deliverables you're responsible for in as much detail as possible. If the client requests work you didn't initially agree on, you can say, "Sure. That will push the deadline to (new date) and the cost to (increased price)." Don't want to do the additional work? Say, "Unfortunately, that wasn't in our original project scope, and I'm at full capacity right now."

493

PLAN YOUR VACATIONS AS FAR OUT AS POSSIBLE. Giving yourself plenty of runway allows you to save up money to replace the income you're not making, plan which projects you'll take on around your time away, and set your clients' expectations on your availability.

494

CREATE A DAILY, WEEKLY, AND MONTHLY ROAD MAP. Disorganized freelancers are burnt-out freelancers. To make sure you never need to pull an all-nighter, map out what you need to accomplish today, this week, and this month. Then do this again the next day, and the day after that, and the day after that...

495

**COMMUNICATE YOUR WORK HOURS TO YOUR CLI-
ENTS.** If your schedule is a mystery, your clients will contact you whenever *they're* available—which means you'll constantly be online. Don't make your schedule a mystery. Here's a handy template: "I'm available for meetings from (X to Y times) on (A to B days). If you call or email me when I'm out (on Fridays, after 4 p.m., etc.), I'll respond ASAP (on Monday morning, the next day)."

496

GET OUTSIDE HELP. This might sound strange as a freelancer, but your time is precious, so outsource as much work as possible. First, calculate your average hourly rate. Then figure out what tasks you're currently doing that someone else could do for "less" (for example, if you spend twenty hours preparing your taxes, effectively losing $4,000, hire an accounting firm to do it for $2,000). You'll have fewer things on your plate *and* save some cash.

497

PERIODICALLY INCREASE YOUR RATES. You'll be able to reduce your client list while making the same amount—maybe more. And it's completely justified; after all, the more experience and expertise you gain, the more your work is worth. Try a 10–20 percent increase every three to six months. Stop raising your rates when you're happy with both your income and your workload.

498

AVOID CLIENTS WHO DON'T KNOW WHAT THEY WANT. The price might sound right, but these projects are always more trouble than they're worth (literally). You'll waste a ton of time and energy trying to figure out their goals, define their vison, and craft a plan—all before getting to the actual work. Undecided clients typically make sudden decisions as well, so you may have to scrap what you've done and take things in a new direction when you're halfway through. When talking to prospective clients, pay close attention to how clearly they can articulate the job. If they're vague or undecided, pass.

499

BLOCK OUT TIME FOR BUSYWORK. That could be every-thing from dealing with administrative tasks to updating your social media to tackling any other business-related work. If you don't schedule these tasks in, you'll end up doing them after your "real work" has been done—in other words, late at night or on the weekends.

500

PRIORITIZE ONGOING CONTRACTS. Every new client comes with a significant amount of work: prospecting for them in the first place, settling on the terms of your contract, figuring out what they're looking for, learning key facts about their goals, and so on. You'll have much more time for billable work if you do multiple projects for one client versus one-off projects for several clients. Set up long-term gigs whenever possible.

501

HIRE A VIRTUAL ASSISTANT (VA). A VA can take a ton of busywork off your plate, from sending invoices and tracking payments to doing preliminary research and keeping your files organized. Hire a VA on *Upwork*, *Fiverr*, *LinkedIn*, or *Zirtual*.

· · ·

502

DO YOUR RESEARCH WHEN JOB HUNTING. When searching for a new job, look for companies that care about work-life balance. It's much easier to stick to the lines you've set between your personal and professional life when your coworkers have set similar lines—and more importantly, your employer respects and supports those lines. To figure out whether this is the case, connect with current and former employees on *LinkedIn* and see if they're willing to share their experience with finding a good work-life balance at that company. Ask how many hours they typically worked per week, how flexible their schedules were, and if their coworkers respected boundaries around vacation and logged-off time. In addition, during the interview process, ask the hiring manager, "Does (company name) have any policies or programs around work-life balance?" and "What are the typical working hours for (this role, similar roles)?" Their answers will give you valuable clues into the company's attitude toward work-life balance.

503

TRY THE FOUR-DAY WORKWEEK. It might sound unconventional, but there's proof it works. Microsoft Japan implemented a four-day workweek in 2019 and saw productivity increase by 40 percent. A firm in New Zealand ran a similar experiment in 2018 and reported productivity was unchanged, attendance was better, employees were more creative, and, best of all, work-life balance rose by 24 percent. Bring these examples to the people who run your company and get their feedback. If you're a freelancer, meaning you call the shots? Give the four-day workweek a go for a month and see how it impacts your output and feelings of work-life balance.

INDEX

IMPROVE YOUR LIFE—
ONE HACK AT A TIME!

Pick Up or Download Your Copies Today!